Education is fundamentally an imaginative act of hope

Inviting School Success

A Self-Concept Approach to Teaching, Learning, and Democratic Practice

Third Edition

This book is dedicated
to our mentor, colleague, and friend:
Hal G. Lewis, an imaginative person of hope.

Inviting School Success

A Self-Concept Approach to Teaching, Learning, and Democratic Practice

Third Edition

William Watson Purkey
The University of North Carolina at Greensboro

John M. Novak
Brock University

Wadsworth Publishing Company
I⟨T⟩P™ An International Thomson Publishing Company

Belmont • Albany • Bonn • Boston • Cincinnati • Detroit • London • Madrid • Melbourne •
Mexico City • New York • Paris • San Francisco • Singapore • Tokyo • Toronto • Washington

Education Editor: Sabra Horne
Assistant Editor: Claire Masson
Editorial Assistant: Louise Mendelson
Production Services Coordinator: Debby Kramer
Production: Robin Gold/Forbes Mill Press
Print Buyer: Karen Hunt
Permissions Editor: Jeanne Bosschart
Interior Design: Robin Gold
Cover Design: Jeanne Calabrese
Copy Editor: Robin Gold
Compositor: Forbes Mill Press
Printer: Malloy Lithographing, Inc.

Acknowledgments

The excerpt on page 112 is reprinted with permission of Macmillan Publishing Co., Inc. and Jonathan Cape Ltd. from *Manchild in the Promised Land* by Claude Brown. Copyright © 1965 by Claude Brown.

The excerpt on page 15 is reprinted with permission of E.P. Dutton & Co., Inc. and Curtis Brown Limited from *Nigger: An Autobiography* by Dick Gregory, with Robert Lipsyte. Copyright © 1964 by Dick Gregory Enterprises, Inc.

The excerpt on pages 130–133 is reprinted with permission of Phi Delta Kappa, Inc. from *By Invitation Only* (Fastback #268) by William W. Purkey and John M. Novak. Copyright © 1988 by the Phi Delta Kappa Educational Foundation.

For more information, contact Wadsworth Publishing Company:

Wadsworth Publishing Company
10 Davis Drive
Belmont, California 94002, USA

International Thomson Publishing Europe
Berkshire House 168-173
High Holborn
London, WC1V 7AA, England

Thomas Nelson Australia
102 Dodds Street
South Melbourne 3205
Victoria, Australia

Nelson Canada
1120 Birchmount Road
Scarborough, Ontario
Canada M1K 5G4

International Thomson Editores
Campos Eliseos 385, Piso 7
Col. Polanco
11560 México D.F. México

International Thomson Publishing GmbH
Königswinterer Strasse 418
53227 Bonn, Germany

International Thomson Publishing Asia
221 Henderson Road
#05-10 Henderson Building
Singapore 0315

International Thomson Publishing Japan
Hirakawacho Kyowa Building, 3F
2-2-1 Hirakawacho
Chiyoda-ku, Tokyo 102, Japan

Library of Congress Cataloging-in-Publication Data
Purkey, William Watson
     Inviting school success : a self-concept approach to teaching, learning, and democratic practice / William Watson Purkey, John M. Novak. — 3rd ed.
       p.   cm.
     Includes bibliographical references and index.
     ISBN 0-534-50419-1 (acid-free paper)
     1. Teaching.   2. Teacher-student relationships.   3. Motivation in education.   I. Novak, John M.   II. Title.
LB1025.2.P89   1996
371.1'02—dc20

95-30505

Contents

Foreword

In this third edition of their popular book, *Inviting School Success*, William Purkey and John Novak state their underlying faith early on: "Education is fundamentally an imaginative act of hope." I agree with them heartily. Today, when pressures toward uniformity are steadily increasing, educators need to hear this message regularly, and they need practical help in exercising imagination so that the hope is kept alive.

Invitational teaching depends heavily on a responsible and caring exercise of imagination. One might suppose that, in its emphasis on perception, invitational teaching requires a suspension of imagination. But teachers who listen carefully in order to discover students' perceptions must then use their imaginations to find ways in which to respond. The standard mode of establishing uniform objectives and forcing them on everyone through repeated use of standard lessons just will not do.

Not only must teachers exercise imagination to find ways of inviting students to learn, they must also use imagination to direct their own perceptions. Purkey and Novak ask us to see students as able, valuable, and responsible. Most young people who choose teaching *do* see students that way, but the initial shock of reality in today's schools can blur their preservice perceptions. An exercise of imagination is needed, not to create a rosy illusion, but to rediscover what is really there.

Inviting School Success is a highly practical book. It is loaded with memorable anecdotes, useful hints, and specific directions. It meticulously describes disinviting and inviting behaviors. In describing unintentionally disinviting behaviors, the authors discuss one such behavior that struck home for me. In my early years as a mathematics teacher, I often said to my students, "Now watch, it's easy!" Purkey and Novak are surely correct when they warn us that such a remark— intended as friendly and reassuring—is in fact disinviting. Students who find a procedure hard, when the teacher has proclaimed it is easy, feel like idiots. I learned to say, "This is hard, but you can do it. It takes prac- tice, but don't worry—I'm here, and I'll help." "This is hard" turns out to be far more inviting than "this is easy." It invites students to try something worthy of their efforts, and it cushions them against the hard blows of occasional failure.

Some critics may raise an objection to *Inviting School Success* that is sometimes raised against my own work on caring. It sounds wonderful, the objection goes, but it won't work today. Maybe this approach worked once-upon-a-time in schools, but schools and kids have changed. Fortu- nately, Purkey and Novak have answered this challenge eloquently. In a chapter aptly titled "Inviting in the Rain" and again in their last two chapters, they show convincingly that invitational teaching is more important now than ever. Their recommendations on an invitational approach to discipline are both theoretically sound and practical; they are *wise* recommendations.

I hope that this third edition will be widely read—that teacher educa- tors will invite their students to read and discuss it, that school adminis- trators will feel invited by the authors, and that they, in turn, will warmly invite their school boards, parents, and teachers to read it also. The reward may be to keep education alive as an imaginative act of hope.

Nel Noddings
Stanford University

Preface

Welcome to this third edition of *Inviting School Success*. This latest edition represents more than a decade of development of what has come to be known as invitational theory. Based on the idea that education is an imaginative act of hope, this theory connects educational activities and democratic practices by demonstrating how everyone and everything in and around classrooms, schools, and the larger culture add to or subtract from the educational experiences individuals and groups construct in their personal and professional lives.

This third edition features developments intended to expand and enrich its value for readers seeking a constructive way of thinking and acting in complex, often tension-filled, educational settings. These developments include

- A new chapter, "Inviting in the Rain," which gives concrete, principled, field-tested strategies for maintaining an inviting stance in the most critical and dangerous times. Highlighted in this chapter are practical steps to create and maintain safe schools.

- A focused theoretical foundation that integrates the perceptual tradition and self-concept theory with key ideas of democratic practice.

- A new chapter, "Creating Inviting Schools," with a blueprint for systematically constructing schools where all want to be, participate, and learn.

- A review of recent research that provides deeper support for applying invitational theory to more aspects of the educative process.

- Numerous ways for educators to avoid compassion fatigue and maintain enthusiasm for teaching, learning, and living.

- A new appendix designed especially for multimedia and communication specialists.

Building on but reaching well beyond the previous editions, this third edition of *Inviting School Success* is more comprehensive and more useful. Looking at the main text in quadrants, the first two chapters show the evolution of invitational education and its theoretical, empirical, and moral base. The next two chapters deal with the particulars of the inviting approach and demonstrate how to systematically apply it. Chapters Five and Six extend the application of invitational thinking to some of the most difficult situations educators face and show how this approach needs to be orchestrated personally and professionally. The final two chapters deal with a vision of schools and society and detail a structured, democratic strategy for bringing this vision to life.

To supply additional strategies for professionals in the field, two appendixes are added. The first provides several hundred suggestions categorized according to ten school roles. The second appendix presents lists of inviting and disinviting signals found in and around schools. These examples are illustrative of concrete ways to begin to make a school more inviting.

We wish to acknowledge those who have contributed to the completion of this latest edition. These include the enthusiastic and ever-helpful staff at Wadsworth: Sabra Horne, Debby Kramer, and Tricia Schumacher. A special acknowledgement to Robin Gold of Forbes Mill Press for her thoughtful approach to the words, ideas, format, and people of this book.

Although it would be impossible to personally thank everyone who has contributed to this third edition of *Inviting School Success*, their contributions are greatly appreciated. Among the many colleagues who provided us with valuable suggestions and support, we would like to particularly thank Terry Boak, Thomas Busnarda, Don Dworet, Bill Evans, Nel Noddings, Peter Paul, John J. Schmidt, David Sherrill, Betty

Siegel, Paula Helen Stanley, William Stafford, Denise Stockley, and Rosemary Young. In addition, we would like to thank the members of the International Alliance for Invitational Education, the American Educational Research Association Special Interest Group on Invititational Education, those who contributed to the *Journal of Invitational Theory and Practice*, and the *Invitational Forum*. We would also like to thank our colleagues who reviewed this book and made helpful suggestions: T.W. Lindenberg, State University of New York, Oswego; A. Michael Dougherty, Western Carolina University; Larry M. Arnoldsen, Brigham Young University; Judy Lehr, Furman University; and Tommie R. Radd, The University of Nebraska at Omaha.

To these colleagues and our loving families, we express our sincere gratitude.

William W. Purkey
John M. Novak

1

Introduction to Invitational Education

In the spring of 1990, Douglas Byrd Junior High School faced a dilemma. The faculty and staff were dedicated and hard-working, but they felt that they were losing the battle against the many challenges they faced. The high dropout and absentee rates were the highest of the 12 junior high schools in Cumberland County, while the scores on standardized tests were the lowest. These and other challenges made Douglas Byrd an excellent testing ground for invitational education.

Inviting School Success describes the theory and practice of invitational education and explains how Douglas Byrd and scores of other schools throughout the United States, Canada, and overseas use this approach in changing the "chemistry" of the school. This book describes what can be done to create similar classrooms and schools. Unlike many educational textbooks that simply survey available research, *Inviting School Success* presents a theory and hands-on information about how to create and maintain schools fitting for an imaginative democratic society.

Education is fundamentally an imaginative act of hope. This hope generates an educational vision and suggests creative means of attainment.

1

Without this, educators become mere technicians and functionaries to a bureaucratic system. Worse yet, they become cynics, going through lifeless motions.

In a democratic social order, there is hope that the educative process can enable all involved to participate in the process of continual self-realization and in the self-rule of their society. For this to happen, we clearly need a hopeful, action-based approach to education.

The authors of this book believe that educators can create and maintain schools that cordially summon all involved in the educative process to value themselves and their abilities, to think more fully and deeply about issues of personal and social concern, and to act imaginatively and caringly in addressing matters of human worth. We contend that educators, as well as everybody and everything involved in the educative process, can—and should—participate in realizing these democratic goals by *inviting* school success.

Just as everyone and everything in hospitals should encourage healing, everyone and everything in schools should invite the realizing of educational goals. This involves the *people* (teachers, administrators, supervisors, counselors, assistants, bus drivers, cafeteria staff, secretaries, librarians, nurses, security guards, custodians, crossing guards), the *places* (classrooms, offices, hallways, commons, restrooms, playing fields, gymnasiums, libraries), the *policies* (rules, codes, procedures), the *programs* (curricular or cocurricular), and the *processes* (the spirit or flavor of the way things are done). The formulation, realization, and evaluation of this concept has been named invitational education. This book offers a theory of practice for its implementation.

The opening chapters of *Inviting School Success* introduce invitational education and describe its theoretical foundations. Later chapters present practical, how-to material that demonstrates ways of translating theory into practice.

What is Invitational Education?

A theory of practice is a way of thinking about that which is considered to be worth doing well. Invitational education is thus a general framework for thinking and acting about what is believed to be worthwhile in schools. As a developing theory of practice, invitational education is incomplete, with questions unanswered and avenues unexplored. Although still evolving, invitational education points in a hopeful direction, offers a systematic approach to the educative process, encourages a common language of improvement, and provides practical ways to make schools "the most inviting places in town."

Invitational education is a democratically oriented, perceptually anchored, self-concept approach to the educative process that centers on five basic principles:

1 People are able, valuable, and responsible and should be treated accordingly.

2 Educating should be a collaborative, cooperative activity.

3 The process is the product in the making.

4 People possess untapped potential in all areas of worthwhile human endeavor.

5 This potential can best be realized by places, policies, programs, and processes specifically designed to invite development and by people who are intentionally inviting with themselves and others personally and professionally.

The five principles of invitational education both focus and constrain educators to operate democratically. First, believing in the ability, value, and responsibility of each person commits educators to developing ethical approaches that summon students to take ownership for their learning. Second, the collaborative, cooperative nature of the teaching/ learning process is emphasized in the "doing-with" nature of inviting. This means that in some meaningful way, teachers and students are "in this thing together." Third, saying "the process is the product in the making" means that how one goes about doing something affects what the result will be. Fourth, the belief in human potential assumes that everyone is only using a small part of his or her many possibilities. Fifth, the idea that every person and everything in and around schools adds to, or subtracts from, the process of being a beneficial presence in the lives of human beings means that people and environments are never neutral; they are either summoning or shunning the development of human potential. Ideally, the factors of people, places, policies, programs, and processes should be so intentionally inviting as to create a world in which each individual is cordially summoned to develop intellectually, socially, physically, psychologically, and morally. This is a lot to expect from all involved in the educative process. To expect less, however, is to diminish hope in people, their potential, and the educative process.

With these principles as a theoretical focal point, the practice of invitational education is based on developing, transmitting, and evaluating caring, proactive messages. Messages are the basic unit in invitational education. Based on an understanding of messages considered/not considered, intended/not intended, extended/not extended, received/not received, evaluated/not evaluated, educational situations are studied, and strategies are suggested, put into practice, and evaluated. With this communicative framework, invitational education proponents can move from the personal to the social by attending to how people talk to themselves and others, think about and develop curriculum, work in schools, and act in and through public institutions (Novak, 1990).

Invitational education provides educators with a systematic and sequential way of looking at messages. This understanding of the depth and breadth of messages is used to develop environments and ways of life that are anchored in attitudes of respect, care, and civility and that encourage the realization of democratic goals. Thus, although invitational education can be applied in many ways, it is not doing whatever feels good; invitational education is a self-correcting system that seeks to integrate—in creative and ethical ways—research, theory, and practice.

The term *invitational education* was chosen because the two words have special meaning. Our English word *invite* is probably a derivative of the Latin word *invitare*, which can mean "to offer something beneficial for consideration." Translated literally, invitare means "to summon cordially, not to shun." The word education comes from the Latin word *educare*, which means to "draw out" or "call forth" something potential or latent. Literally, then, invitational education is the process by which people are cordially summoned to realize their potential in all areas of worthwhile human endeavor.

The concept of potential, as Israel Scheffler (1985) pointed out, is essential for a thorough understanding of education. Potential, as used in invitational education, is not some preformed destiny existing within the individual. Rather, potential refers to the energies and interests of people that can be connected to worthwhile opportunities that encourage refinement and further possibilities for growth. With this view of potential in mind, invitational education practitioners work toward developing caring behaviors, nurturing environments, person-centered policies, engaging programs, and democratic processes. These people aim to create an educational culture that summons everyone involved to become lifelong learners.

What, then, is invitational education? Although this entire book is an answer to this question, this opening chapter provides a brief overview of invitational education's development and presents an explanation of some of invitational education's basic concepts and principles. Various aspects of invitational education, along with practical applications, are presented throughout this book.

The Development of Invitational Education

Invitational education is an evolving theory of practice. This section highlights the evolutionary development that has occurred since its inception in the 1970s. This development can be represented as three generations of thinking about invitational education that are reflected in the three editions (1978, 1984, 1996) of *Inviting School Success*.

First Generation Thinking

The first generation of thinking about invitational education (Purkey, 1978) attempted to define a systematic way of promoting the development of positive and realistic self-concepts in students. (The importance of student self-concept and its relation to success or failure in life will be explored in Chapter Two.) This initial thinking focused on the teacher—his or her attentiveness, expectations, attitudes, perspectives, and evaluations—as the primary force influencing students' perceptions of themselves.

Reports on the impact of the actions of significant others on self-concept and behavior were reported from professions other than teaching.

For example, the field of medicine recognized that certain sicknesses (iatrogenic diseases) can result from the physician's witting or unwitting signals to patients to consider themselves less than healthy (*Dorland's*, 1974). Also cited was research in clinical psychology that emphasized that improved behavior results from therapy primarily because of the relationship's attitudinal qualities, which encourage a positive, realistic self-concept in clients (Rogers, 1973, 1974). This perspective is perhaps best exemplified by a client who wrote, "It was not what he knew, but who he was, that seemed to help me the most." First generation thinking about invitational education concluded that, at heart, the teaching-learning process is a collaborative, cooperative activity. Trying to make students learn without their purposes being considered was seen as a lost cause. Rather than spending energy trying to build, enhance, modify, shape, reinforce, make, turn on, motivate, or whatever, invitational education views education as a "doing-with" as opposed to a "doing-to" process. Simply stated, invitational education proponents proposed that teachers seek ways to summon students cordially to participate in realizing their many positive potentials. Thus, the first generation thinking about invitational education considered the effects of attitudes and behaviors on human functioning with the purpose of advocating more intentional and dependable invitational classroom practices.

Second Generation Thinking

The second edition of *Inviting School Success* (Purkey & Novak, 1984) extended the scope of invitational education. Although reaffirming that teaching was basically an inviting process, everyone and everything in and around schools were identified as signal systems that invite or disinvite success in schools. Schools were seen as functional wholes in which the parts influence the whole and the whole affects the parts.

In practice, invitational education addressed the five powerful "P's" that constitute any school: People, Places, Policies, Programs, and Processes. Examples of invitational education in action are *people* in schools who always call others by their preferred names, *places* that are clean and aesthetically pleasing, *policies* that open schools early to get students away from icy wind, *programs* that include all students, and *processes* that are democratically and ethically defensible. Educators have the responsibility to systematically think about, and construct, learning environments that dependably and imaginatively communicate that students are able, valuable, and responsible and can behave accordingly.

During second generation thinking, invitational education moved to more complex patterns of action. The inviting process was seen as reciprocal in nature; individuals and groups are continually interacting: sending/not sending, accepting/not accepting. Thus, the countless choices people make regarding when, what, and how to send and receive invitations become an integral and complex part of the process.

In addition, areas for inviting oneself and others, personally and professionally, were identified. Inviting is not limited to professional settings. Rather, it is a way of approaching all relationships that does justice to the uniqueness of the people involved. Personal and professional lives are not hermetically sealed compartments existing in splendid isolation. Real lives are connected wholes. Invitational education acknowledges the richness, complexities, and possibilities inherent in these connections and attempts to deal with them in a caring and coherent way.

Third Generation Thinking

Since the publication of the second edition of *Inviting School Success*, invitational education has been enriched by the publication of numerous books, monographs, and research papers and by the biannual academic publication, *The Journal of Invitational Theory and Practice*. This has been accomplished by the growth of the International Alliance for Invitational Education with more than 1,000 members and annual conferences since 1982. These activities have extended invitational education beyond classrooms and school systems to even larger areas of human interaction. In so doing, the foundations of invitational education have been updated and deepened, and some of the most challenging personal, professional, and social issues have been considered from an inviting framework. At this point it is helpful to return to the question "What is invitational education?" to explain its expanded range.

Invitational education is a *theory of practice*. If theory is a way of thinking about something and practice is that which is worth doing well, a theory of practice is a way of thinking about that which is worth doing well. Invitational education enables educators to do it better—to more deeply participate in the interactions, ideals, and rewards of teaching. As a theory of practice, invitational education provides an integrative and self-correcting framework for suggesting principles and plans of action to educators.

The principles and plans of action suggested by invitational education represent a *democratically oriented, perceptually based, self-concept approach* to teaching and learning. Democracy—as Lappé and DuBois (1994), Novak (1994), Stuhr (1993), and others see it—is more than a political system; it is also an ethical ideal that aims at constructing ways of living in which people have the interests, abilities, and opportunities to grow and participate in their self-rule.

As an ideal, democracy involves a deep and abiding commitment to the idea that those who are affected by decisions should have a say in the formulation, implementation, and evaluation of these decisions. Implied here is a faith in people being able to articulate and act intelligently upon issues that confront their common life. Also implied is that people close to the issues have something important to offer. The ideal of democracy is a "doing-with" approach to people at all levels. In addition, participating in democratic practices is also an important educational means and ends because it is a vital way to develop intellectual and social potential (Westbrook, 1991). People can become smarter and more connected by learning to participate in constructing the common goods of social life.

Why Invitational Education?

These are challenging times in education. Educators are pressured to do more, with less, and do it even better. As is often the case during times of great challenge, it is easy to lose sight of valued goals and merely ask for a redoubling of effort. This frenzied pressure is taking its toll as more and more teachers express second thoughts about their vocational choice, counselors experience "compassion fatigue," and principals report "disillusionment" (Carnegie Foundation for the Advancement of Teaching, 1991).

Invitational education redirects the energy of current challenges to schooling by reconnecting with the hopes of educators, by heading educational practices in a defensible and consistent direction, and by offering strategies for handling difficult situations. To do this, we must work from a language that expresses care.

Caring is an ethic that guides action (Gilligan, 1982; Gilligan, Ward & Taylor, 1988; Gilligan, Lyons & Hammer, 1990; Noddings, 1984, 1986, 1992; Prillaman, Eaker & Kendrich, 1994). Caring is reflected through "modeling, dialogue, practice, and confirmation" (Noddings, 1986, p. 502). Invitational education provides a language that expresses care and a practice that exhibits it.

A Language That Expresses Care

We speak with words;
but words are not just uttered,
they are chosen.
We use a language;
but that language is not merely words,
it is a unique way of choosing to be in the world.
We teach others a way of being in the world;
but they are not mere recipients,
they also choose to show us their lives and hopes.

Teaching is a delicate and precious relationship. The words used to describe teaching are not neutral because words involve choices, perspectives, and hopes. These in turn affect what people see, think, and do. Unfortunately educators have often chosen words and conceptual systems that violate the integrity of people and the educative process.

Many words used to describe teaching are based on a "doing-to" relationship. Teachers are directed to motivate, reinforce, build, shape, enhance, and turn on students. As well-intentioned as these directions may be, they are fundamentally misguided. Students are not passive recipients who can be turned on and cranked out. They are active participants in the process of trying to construct a life. A "doing-to" language is metaphorically appropriate for working with machines, not people.

The metaphor of "teaching as inviting" was developed in response to these concerns. Based on the idea of a "doing-with" relationship, teaching creatively calls forth participation in beneficial activities, and learning is fundamentally connected to a person's intrinsic motive to seek meaning in the world. As used here, an *inviting message* is a summary description of those communications—transmitted by people, places, policies, programs, or processes—that present something beneficial for consideration and acceptance. Inviting messages are intended to inform people that they are able, valuable, and responsible; that they have opportunities to participate in their own development; and that they are cordially summoned to take advantage of these opportunities. Conversely, a *disinviting message* informs its recipients that they are irresponsible, incapable, and worthless and that they cannot participate in activities of any significance. An inviting message is an effort to establish a cooperative interaction; a disinviting message is an effort to establish a controlling or negating interaction. Inviting and disinviting messages take countless forms and deal with all human relationships. Their presence has been documented by Inglis (1976), Lambeth (1980), Turner (1982), Amos (1985), Radd (1988), Chance (1992), Stanley and Purkey (1995), and others. People are surrounded by these messages, from formal requests to informal urgings, from verbal comments to nonverbal behaviors, from official policies and programs to unwritten rituals and agendas. Individually and collectively, these messages play a significant role in determining what happens in schools.

An inviting message may be as formal as a bronze pin presented at an assembly awards program, an assignment to a special project, or a complimentary note sent to parents. It may also be as informal as a teacher taking special notice of a child's new shoes, as subtle as providing a cough drop for a nagging cough, or as nonverbal as a smile, nod, pat, or wink. Even several seconds of silence ("wait-time") at the right moment can be most inviting.

The Power of Invitations

Everything the teacher does as well as the manner in which he does it incites the child to respond in some way or another and each response tends to set the child's attitude in some way or another.

John Dewey, *How We Think* (1933, p. 59)

Current research evidence is scarce, but we can hypothesize that individuals have a basic need to be noticed, and noticed favorably, by others. As William James (1890) commented long ago, "No more fiendish punishment could be devised, were such a thing possible, than that one should be turned loose in society and remain absolutely unnoticed by all the members thereof" (p. 179). This basic need for affirmation has also been described by Martin Buber: "Man wishes to be confirmed in his being by man, and wishes to have a presence in the being of the other . . . secretly and bashfully he watches for a Yes which allows him to be and which can come only from one human person to another. It is from one person to another that the heavenly bread of self-being is passed" (1965, p. 71). Thus, from James's and Buber's perspective, individuals help create one another.

Following James's and Buber's thinking, it appears that no one is self-made. Each day students are influenced by the way the school bus driver greets them as they step on the bus, by the policies established by the school board, by the way the food is prepared and served in the cafeteria. They are also influenced by the ways the physical environment is maintained, by the way classes are conducted, and by the nature and availability of programs. *Everything* in the school counts, either positively or negatively.

Of all the things that count, nothing is as important as the people in the process. Teaching machines, microcomputers, programmed materials, distance learning, communication highways, and other technological advances may play an important role in education, but they cannot substitute for human relationships. Teaching is a way of being with people. This "being-with" process has a great impact on students' ideas about themselves and their abilities.

Even more than "being with," invitational education suggests a bidding to go somewhere, to see people not only as they are, but also as they might become, to look ahead to tomorrow's promise. Most educators who have been in schools awhile understand the importance of having a positive vision of the future. An elementary school teacher wrote,

> *In my second-grade class I had each child express what he or she*
> *would like to be as an adult. After listening to each child, I said:*
> *"Everybody look up at your star in the sky and reach for it!" Every*

child in the room started reaching as high as possible. The amazing thing is that they all wanted to learn something each day just so I could say to them: "Reach up and see if you're a little bit closer to your star."

Each human watches closely for clues in the behavior of others. A teacher's verbal and nonverbal signals that the student is able, valuable, and responsible can be marvelously reassuring to a child struggling with a difficult spelling word, a complex math problem, a threatening oral report, or an effort to reach a star. Successful teachers realize that humans are in a constant process of being created. They use this realization to develop appropriate and caring patterns of communication.

Patterns of Communication

Inviting the development of human potential is highly complex. Life's whispered invitations are often intangible and can be so subtle and indirect that individuals are sometimes unaware of their effects. A certain pattern exists, however, in the endless variety of messages transmitted in and around schools. When this pattern is brought into focus, previously unexamined factors can be identified that result in students feeling invited or disinvited in school.

Feeling Invited

During the past decade, thousands of students at various academic levels have provided the authors with examples of inviting or disinviting messages they received during their years of schooling. The great majority of students of various ages remember clearly what it was like to feel invited in school. Their illustrations fell into one of three categories: (1) able, (2) valuable, and (3) responsible.

Able

"Mr. Mac said I had made the most progress of anyone in the class."

"I remember my science teacher saying I was a careful researcher."

"My teacher asked me if she could take a copy of my paper to show at a teacher workshop."

"She was enthusiastic about my poetry and arranged to have it entered in a contest."

"Coach said I had natural ability."

"Mrs. Warren would write 'tres bon' on our papers when she was pleased."

"My English teacher, Mr. Maras, always said: 'Be great!' And he meant it."

Valuable

"Mr. Evans cared enough to come to school a half hour early each morning just to help me with science."

"The teacher treated us like we were somebody. I recall the time she invited all of us to her home for a cookout."

"The first day of school my teacher said she was going to teach me how to smile, and she did."

"The principal always remembered my name."

"I could tell the counselor was genuinely interested in me. She listened."

"When I was in the hospital, my teacher came to visit."

Responsible

"Coach asked me to take the equipment out and explain the rules."

"She didn't try to force us to work, but she made it clear that we would hurt ourselves by goofing off."

"When I decided to choose French over Spanish, I could tell that the Spanish teacher respected my decision."

"She let us do something on our own; she trusted us."

"I remember my third-grade teacher telling me how proud she was of our behavior during her absence—she said we were like sixth-graders!"

Again and again, students reported that certain teachers had a flair for inviting. They felt that their teachers were partners in learning. One student wrote, "Whenever I was in Miss Penn's English class, I could feel myself becoming more intelligent!" In light of these comments it is not surprising that students learn best when placed in the care of educators who invite them to see themselves as able, valuable, and responsible and to behave accordingly.

Unfortunately, many students describe memories of their schooling that center on feelings of being worthless, incapable, and irresponsible. When asked to describe the messages they received in school, these students reported feelings of being disinvited.

Feeling Disinvited

Many students explained that they felt disinvited in school simply because they were consistently overlooked. They said they were seldom encouraged to participate in school activities, that they rarely played on a team, belonged to a club, held an office, attended a school function, or were even called on in class. They stated that they did not feel a part of school and that they seldom related with faculty and staff in even the most casual way. Their teachers usually returned papers without comment except for a letter grade, and they rarely seemed to notice the students' absences from school. These students suffered from a "caring disability"; not enough educators cared to invite them to participate in school life.

Perhaps the time will come when schools, like hospitals, will have "Intensive Care" programs for those who need special help. If students are to succeed in school, they must have an environment that nurtures their potential. When they are treated with indifference, they are likely to become indifferent to themselves and to school. They begin to say to themselves, "Give up, no one cares about your small victories." This general process has been described by Willis (1970) as systematic extinction. What it means for the educator is that students who have learned to deny their abilities as learners are vulnerable to failure, just as physically weak people are susceptible to illness.

Adding to the problem of indifferent treatment, students who constantly feel disinvited may decide to seek revenge. Most students are acutely aware when some are given more opportunities and encouragement than others. "They feel there's a party going on and they haven't been invited." Those who feel disinvited remember keenly the slights they receive.

Many students are disinvited by educators who, either intentionally or unintentionally, behave in ways that result in student embarrassment, frustration, and failure. A high-school girl wrote,

> *My Latin teacher did not like females, particularly "socially oriented" ones. And I met both requirements. I was in a room with my best friends, which included males and females. The teacher would pick me out and have me go to the board and write something in Latin. Of course, when I missed something, which was often, the entire class got a lecture on studying more and socializing less. But I had to stand in front of the class by myself the entire time while the lecture on the evils of "socializing" was being presented. I was usually so embarrassed I would end up crying in the bathroom where no one could see me.*

Canfield and Wells (1976) use the term "killer statements" to describe the means by which a student's feelings, thoughts, and creativity are "killed off" by another person's negative comments, physical gestures, or other behaviors. Esquiriel (1992) referred to these individuals as "frigid breath" people. Their very presence can dash optimism and hope, and their actions can be lethal. These actions may be little more than a teacher's suddenly stiffened spine when a child of another race touches his or her arm—or as elusive as the failure to call on or even look at certain children.

A child's feelings of being disinvited are described by Dick Gregory in his autobiography *Nigger* (1964): "The teacher thought I was a trouble-maker. All she saw from the front of the room was a little black boy who squirmed in his idiot's seat and made noises and poked the kids around him. I guess she couldn't see a kid who made noises because he wanted someone to know he was there" (p. 30). Whether intentional or unintentional, disinviting messages can have long-lasting effects.

Students who reported that they felt disinvited in school described experiences that could be divided into three categories of self-perception: (1) worthless, (2) unable, and (3) irresponsible. Here are some examples.

Worthless

"On the first day of school, the teacher came in and said he wasn't supposed to teach this basic class, but that he was stuck with us."

"My name is Bill Dill, but the teacher always called me 'Dill Pickle' and laughed."

"One teacher told me I just wanted to cause trouble all the time."

"The teacher said 'That's crazy! What's the matter with you?' His negative attitude toward me stood out like a bump on your nose."

"I transferred to a new school after it had started. When I appeared at the teacher's doorway, she said 'Oh, no, not another one!'"

"My teacher told me I was the worst kid she ever taught."

Unable

"They put me in the dummy class, and it had *Special Education* painted right on the door."

"The teacher said to me in front of the whole class: 'I really don't think you're that stupid.'"

"The principal showed me to the visitor as an example of a 'slow child' who could 'dress nice.'"

"When the principal hit me with a paddle, he said it was the only language I understood."

"They kept telling me I got to learn to keep my mouth shut and stay in my seat."

"I was asked if I had enough sense to follow simple directions."

Irresponsible

"The teacher said I had to be watched every minute."

"She said I was worse than my brother, and I don't even have a brother."

"Because I failed to bring my homework, the teacher asked me why I bothered coming to school."

"She told the class we were discipline problems and were not to be trusted."

"The teacher put me out in the hall for everyone to laugh at."

"The coach told me he couldn't count on me for anything important."

Of course, negative experiences may spur someone to future success, but this is likely to be true only of students who do not easily accept rejection and failure. Students who fight back against disinviting experiences do so only because they have a history of invitations received, accepted, and successfully acted upon. They have built up a partial immunity to failure. Students who readily accept disinviting messages about themselves and their abilities are usually those who have been infected with failure early in life. As one student wrote, "Hell, how can I feel good about myself when I'm stuck in the dummy class year after year?" Research by Roderick (1994) demonstrates the impact of early failure on later school performance. She reported that students who are forced to repeat a grade from kindergarten to sixth grade are far more likely to drop out of school later even when differences in background and post retention grades are controlled. Being retained and thus being overage for a grade during adolescence may explain the higher dropout rate for failed students.

The picture drawn from countless descriptions is that students live in a world of attitudes, expectancies, and evaluations. The full impact of this world has yet to be determined, but it seems clear that student success or failure is related to the ways in which students perceive themselves and their environments—and that these perceptions are influenced by the prevailing nature of the messages they receive in school.

Summary

This opening chapter introduced invitational education and explained how it serves as a vehicle for understanding the influence of people, places, policies, programs, and processes on students. Some students are invited to learn, some are overlooked, and some are dissuaded. These memories can be retained for many years, as the statements from students demonstrated. Evidence was presented that individuals respond best when they share the company of educators who believe them to be able, valuable, and responsible and who intentionally summon them to share in these beliefs. This is an important approach to schooling in and for a democratic society. Chapter Two offers a detailed look at the foundations of invitational education.

2

Foundations of Invitational Education

Human behavior is always a product of how people see themselves and the situations in which they are involved. Although this fact seems obvious, the failure of people everywhere to comprehend it is responsible for much of human misunderstanding, maladjustment, conflict and loneliness. Our perceptions of ourselves and the world are so real to us that we seldom pause to doubt them.

A.W. Combs, D. Avila, and W.W. Purkey, *Helping Relationships: Basic Concepts for the Helping Professions,* **Second Edition (1978, p. 15)**

Any approach to education is based on certain assumptions about what people are like and what they might become. This chapter considers three cornerstone assumptions of invitational education: the perceptual tradition, self-concept theory, and democratic practice.

The Perceptual Tradition

Invitational education has its roots in the perceptual approach to understanding human behavior. Rather than viewing people as objects to be shaped, reinforced, and conditioned, or as captives of unconscious urges or unfulfilled desires, the perceptual tradition views people as they typically see themselves, others, and the world. The starting point is the notion that each person is a conscious agent: He or she experiences, interprets, constructs, decides, acts, and is ultimately responsible for his or her actions.

Historically, many have contributed to the perceptual approach. The long list includes the following:

- William James's description of consciousness (1890)
- George Herbert Mead's perspective on the social nature of perception (1934)
- Prescot Lecky's notion of the consistent nature of perceptions (1945)
- George Kelly's development of personal constructs as the basis of perceptions (1955)
- Gordon Allport's (1937, 1943, 1955, 1961) and Carl Rogers's (1947, 1951, 1959, 1965, 1969, 1974, 1980) career-long emphases on people as perceptive, purposeful, and capable of taking responsibility for their present lives and future aspirations
- Sidney Jourard's use of the concept of self-disclosure (1967, 1968, 1971)
- William Powers's connection of perception and systems theory (1973)
- Martin Seligman's explanation of learned helplessness (1975) and learned optimism (1990)
- Donald Meichenbaum's cognitive behavior modification (1977)
- Robert Kegan's exploration of the evolving nature of meaning-making and perception (1982)
- Albert Bandura's social cognitive theory (1986)
- Walter Truett Anderson's (1990) description of postmodern beliefs and behavior.

Educational researchers have taken seriously this turning to the person's perspective through the growing use and refinement of qualitative research methods to investigate perceptions (Bogdan & Biklen, 1992; Denzin, 1989; Eisner, 1991; Goldman, 1989; Guba, 1990; Krumboltz, 1986; Lichtenberg, 1986; Moustakas, 1990). The perceptual tradition will have an increasingly important role in understanding human behavior.

Invitational education builds on the perceptual tradition and places special emphasis on the Snygg-Combs theory of perception. First presented in 1949 by Donald Snygg and Arthur Combs, this theory has been revised several times (Combs & Snygg, 1959; Combs, Richards & Richards, 1976) and applied to teacher education (Combs, 1982; Combs, Blume, Newman & Wass, 1974) and to the helping professions in general (Combs, Avila & Purkey, 1978; Combs, 1989; Combs & Gonzalez, 1994). The basic contention of this theory is that people behave according to how they see themselves and the situations in which they are involved (Combs et al., 1978). Because of this emphasis on understanding and working with people as they normally see themselves and the world, perceptual theory seems well suited for use in many professional settings, including teaching, administering, counseling, nursing, and related human service activities.

Three assumptions of the perceptual tradition follow, along with examples of how each supports invitational education.

Behavior Is Based on Perceptions

The perceptual tradition seeks to explain why people do the things they do by postulating that human behavior is determined by, and pertinent to, the phenomenal field of the experiencing person at the moment of acting. In other words, each individual behaves according to how the world appears at that instant. From this vantage point, there is no such thing as illogical behavior—every person is behaving in the way that makes the most sense to her or him at that particular instant. What may seem illogical from an external point of view, and even upon reflection from an internal viewpoint, is only an inadequate understanding of what the world looks like from the internal viewpoint of the behaving person at the moment of action.

Perhaps a personal example can clarify this. Several years ago one of the authors of this book was trying to learn to hang glide. He had soloed an airplane and knew the basic rule of aerodynamics: "Thou shalt always maintain thy airspeed or thou shalt smite the ground." However, when he was taking his first "easy" flight in a hang glider that was not designed to take him more than five feet off the ground, he got caught by an updraft and was suddenly thirty-five feet high. At that moment, rather than level-ing off as he had been taught, he closed his eyes and pushed the frame of the kite away from his body and promptly climbed to sixty feet! Some-how, through a series of fortunate events, he returned to earth without being killed.

Why did he close his eyes and push the frame forward when he knew the consequences of such an action? There are various explanations for his behavior, each with its defenders. A behaviorist might conclude that he had been insufficiently reinforced in the standard way of leveling the frame and thus had not been properly conditioned to emit the correct response. A Freudian might hypothesize that perhaps he had an uncon-scious death wish and that his behavior was a manifestation of this basic impulse. A perceptualist, by comparison, would try to "read behavior backwards," to discover what the world looked like to the student pilot the moment he closed his eyes and pushed the frame forward. In looking back at the incident, the novice was totally surprised to be up so high so soon. At that moment he could think of nothing else but to do the safest thing he could—to close his eyes and get the frame as far away from him-self as fast as possible. His reasoning then was, "If I can't see the ground, it can't hurt me." Later, such thinking seemed absurd. At the instant of behaving, however, closing his eyes and pushing away the frame made the most sense. Threat narrows perception and reduces differentiations.

As used here, *perception* refers to the differentiations a person is able to make in his or her personal world of experience. In the hang glider example, the threatened person had a severely restricted perceptual field called tunnel vision (Combs et al., 1978). Tunnel vision is triggered by real or imagined threat. Because of threat, and thus a restricted perceptual field, he could make only limited differentiations.

As further evidence of the power of perception, alcohol consumption appears to be used by social drinkers and alcoholics alike to reduce per-ceptions of personal failure (Hull & Young, 1993). As Taylor (1989) pointed out, clarity can be quite painful at times.

The perceptual tradition holds that to understand human behavior you must make sense of how things appear from the vantage point of the individual perceiver at the moment of behaving. From the perceptual point of view, the fundamental unit of analysis is the way an experiencing human being views oneself, others, and the world at a particular moment in time.

The perceptual tradition implies that there is much more to the world than what is presently perceived. This has been well documented by Gardner (1991), who has shown that people lock into perceptions developed early in life. These intuitive perceptions can block out more complex processes of the world, processes that can be understood by sustained disciplined inquiry.

Fortunately, each person's perceptual field can be continually enriched, expanded, and modified. The ideas that individuals can enhance their perceptions and that their perceptual fields are capable of incalculable expansion and modification serve as major reasons for invitational education. Without such a belief in human development, invitational education would be very limited. Such a belief provides something to continually appreciate and reach for: a coming together for creative, worthwhile purposes that can extend human experiences.

Perceptions Are Learned

No one reading these words was born with the perceptions he or she presently possesses. Perceptions change over time. Through myriad encounters with the world, particularly those with significant others, people develop certain fundamental perceptions that serve as organizing filters for making sense of the world. Without such a filtering system, each person would be relentlessly bombarded by unrelated stimuli, creating an infinitely chaotic existence. Without an organized "in here," there could be no organized "out there."

Perceptions serve as a reference point for behavior. They influence the memories people use to understand the present and anticipate the future. In addition, perceptions affect the possibilities that people can imagine and the goals that they are willing to work for. Thus, any change in perceptions alters one's view of the past, present, future, and the imaginable.

Invitational education is based on an understanding of, and respect for, people's perceptual worlds. These perceptual worlds are not to be taken lightly, for they provide the basis for meaning and behavior. How sensitive educators are to how people perceive themselves, others, and the world affects the messages they choose to extend and accept. Fortunately, sensitivity to the perceptual worlds of oneself and others can be enhanced through reflection.

Perceptions Can Be Reflected Upon

The ability to examine one's perceptions is essential to invitational education. Being aware of past and present perceptions and being able and willing to go beyond them permit the development of a deeper level of understanding of self, others, and the world. As Csikszentmihalyi (1993) points out, reflection can lead a person to develop a more differentiated and integrated self, that is, a personality with many interests creatively harmonized.

Reflection also provides a basis for hope because there is no inevitable future as long as people are willing to rethink perceptions of the past and apply this thinking to different aspects of their lives. Although people cannot change the past, they can change their perceptions of previous events and consequently open more possibilities in the future. For this to work, it is important to savor present perceptions and imaginatively project these perceptions, and the means of their attainment, into the future. This then involves a sense of the aesthetic and instrumental aspects of the perceptual process (Kupfer, 1983). As a colleague, Bill Stafford, noted, invitational education is based on more than "I feel"; it is also "I think," "I know," "I reflect," "I imagine."

This chapter, thus far, has emphasized that people behave according to how they perceive themselves, others, and the world; that these perceptions are learned; and that they can be reflected upon. Now, please consider what is a vital perception for each individual: perception of oneself.

Self-Concept Theory

You see, really and truly, apart from the things anyone can pick up (the dressing and the proper way of speaking, and so on), the difference between a lady and a flower girl is not how she behaves, but how she's treated. I shall always be a flower girl to Professor Higgins, because he treats me as a flower girl, and always will; but

I know I can be a lady to you, because you always treat me as a lady, and always will.

Eliza Doolittle to Colonel Pickering,
George Bernard Shaw, *Pygmalion* (1940, p. 80)

Of all the perceptions people learn, none seems to affect one's search for personal significance and identity more than self-perception—a person's view of who one is and how one fits in the world.

Some theorists (Combs & Gonzalez, 1994; Combs et al., 1978; Rogers, 1947, 1951, 1967; Snygg & Combs, 1949) have postulated that the maintenance, protection, and enhancement of the perceived self (one's own personal existence as viewed by oneself) is the basic motive behind all human behavior. Use of this basic assumption, organized into what is generally known as self-concept theory, can clarify and integrate seemingly unrelated aspects of life in classrooms. For example, students who have learned to see themselves as troublemakers may respond by being discipline problems, just as students who have learned to view themselves as scholars may spend many hours in libraries. The dynamics are the same, even if the resulting behaviors are quite different.

Although disagreeing about the direction of causality, numerous researchers (Darakjian, Michael & Knapp-Lee, 1985; Hansford & Hattie, 1982; Harter, 1983; Hattie, 1992) have demonstrated a modest but positive relationship between self-concept and academic achievement. Researchers consistently agree that there is a relationship between students' evaluations of themselves and their level of academic achievement (Byrne, 1984, 1986; Chapman, 1988; Eshel & Klein, 1981; Harper & Purkey, 1993; Hoge & Renzulli, 1993). Students who have more positive perceptions of themselves and their abilities are more persistent at school tasks (Chapman, 1988), whereas those who have poor self-concepts are more likely to give up when faced with difficult situations (Covington, 1984). Colangelo, Kelly, and Schrepfer (1987) reported their general findings that self-concept and academic ability are related. Understanding self-concept and its relation to invitational education is advantageous for educators who wish to function in a professionally inviting manner.

Self-concept has served as a central part of many human personality theories and the basis for numerous programs in education. Led by the early pathfinding research and writings of Lecky (1945), Raimy (1948),

Rogers (1951, 1967), Combs and Snygg (1959), Patterson (1961), Wylie (1961, 1974, 1979), Diggory (1966), Coopersmith (1967), Fitts and Hamner (1969), and many others, investigators have gathered a large body of empirical data on self-concept. More recently, Seeman (1988) and Hattie (1992) have documented a remarkable resurgence of interest in the self. The emerging literature is so vast that this chapter can examine only four aspects of self-concept that relate most directly to invitational education: (1) self-concept development, (2) self-concept as a guidance system, (3) the significance of positive self-regard, and (4) efforts to promote positive self-concept in students.

Self-Concept Development

No one is born with a self-concept. The development and structure of self-awareness is a lifelong research project. The ever-widening experiences of the developing person constantly modify the self-concept. By experiencing the world through inviting and disinviting interactions with others, as well as through interactions with oneself, the developing person organizes a theory of personal existence.

Each person learns early to identify oneself with categories (for example, female, African-American, Southerner, Canadian, Methodist, Virginian, and so forth) and with attributes (for example, good, bad, strong, weak, valuable, worthless, responsible, irresponsible, able, unable, and so on). Harter (1983, 1988) proposed that self-concept consists of domains that differ in significance for the individual according to one's age. Some domains are more significant at certain ages than others. For example, job performance, social competence, and appearance are self-concept components that are salient factors in defining the self in adulthood.

Through countless interactions with the world, each individual gradually forges a self-concept, complete with a complex hierarchy of attributes and categories. Marsh (1993) developed a schema that divides self-concept into components, including academic self-concept and social self-concept. In addition, he studied math self-concept and school self-concept.

The ingredients of self-concept are primarily social, obtained through countless interactions with persons, places, policies, programs, and processes. As a way of interpreting oneself, each individual attributes meaning to the acts of others. For example, one child announced at the dinner table that she was an honest person. When asked how she knew she was honest, she replied, "Because my teacher asked me to help her grade papers!" Children learn to see themselves as honest just as they learn to view themselves as dishonest. The self-concepts of students are heavily influenced by those who treat them as able, valuable, and responsible—as well as by those who treat them as unable, worthless, and irresponsible. At some level of awareness each person continually asks a very basic question: "Who do you say I am?" The answer to this question influences how people behave and what they become.

Beginning early in life, infants receive countless cues as to their value in the eyes of significant others. Adults communicate these cues to the infant through their postures, facial expressions, gestures, eye contact, and other body movements as well as through their vocalizations.

Words are always accompanied by gestures that elucidate, emphasize, enhance, or even contradict the spoken word. The father who says to his small child "Of course I love you" while his eyes never leave the television set, or the teacher who speaks of her high regard for students, but shivers inside at their touch, contradict their words with their behavior. What people do speaks much louder than what they say. This is particularly true in schools, where inviting or disinviting messages can be recognized in every aspect of school life.

Next to the home, schools probably exert the single greatest influence on how students see themselves and their abilities. According to Patterson, "The concepts which the teacher has of the children become the concepts which the children come to have of themselves" (1973, p. 125). Of course, the child is constantly construing the environment and affects it as well as being affected by it (Piaget, 1973). There is a continuous and constant interaction between the child and the school.

Most public school students spend more than a thousand hours per year in school. Their experiences in school play a major role in determining what they think of themselves and their abilities. One student described a school experience this way:

When I was in the fifth grade, we had a variety show every Friday afternoon. One Friday I sang a song. My teacher loved the song because her husband was in the military and far away. The song was about "Sending myself to my loved one in a letter." I have always tried to please my teachers, but never have I pleased anyone so much! She embraced me, both physically and psychologically, and invited me to sing before the PTA. I've been singing ever since!

Of all the contemporary models of teaching, none depends more on the teacher's personal and professional qualities than does invitational education. Classroom teachers, as Beane (1991) and others stressed, are stimulus objects, attractive or repellent in their own right. By their very presence, they have a subtle but profound impact on students' self-concepts. The teacher's task, therefore, is to behave in ways that encourage positive perceptions in students regarding themselves and their abilities.

From the moment students first make contact with school, the inviting or disinviting actions of school personnel—coupled with the physical environments, the official policies, the instructional programs, and the political processes—dominate their education. Students able to meet the academic expectations of schools are likely to develop positive attitudes toward themselves as learners, whereas those who fail are likely to develop negative feelings. Clearly, school profoundly influences students' development.

Unfortunately, a significant decrease in both self-regard and attitudes toward school and academics apparently occurs with advances in age and grade level. For example, students' positive attitudes toward writing decline steadily and significantly across the grades. According to the United States Department of Education (1987), in the fourth grade, 57 percent of the students report that they like to write. By the eleventh grade this has declined to 39 percent.

Studies have indicated a downward trend in student self-concept as students progress through school (Griffore & Bianchi, 1984; Harper & Purkey, 1993; Silvernail, 1987). Marsh (1993) reported that academic self-concept dropped for both boys and girls from grades four through seven. Harper and Purkey (1993) researched differences in self-concept-as-learner among average and gifted boys and girls in grades six through eight. They found a downward spiral in both inferred and professed self-concept-as-learner of both boys and girls and both gifted and average students. This study was supported by Stanley (1991b, 1993) who reported downward trends in self-concept-as-learner of junior high school students representing both gender and racial groups.

The following exemplifies how the slippage might occur: "I hate poetry," one student explained. "I remember when we misbehaved we had to stay after school and memorize a poem. I never developed anything but a bitter taste for poetry." This gradual erosion of enthusiasm for learning provides a compelling argument for more inviting schools. Based on their longitudinal study of 175 middle-level students, Stanley and Purkey (1995) reported that students who are surrounded by an inviting environment are not as likely to experience a decline in self-concept-as-learner as students in less intentionally supportive schools.

In addition to the downward trend in student self-concept, significant differences have been reported among the variables of gender and race. Studies have produced conflicting results. Although the emerging research on gender and race is conflicting, many continuing inequities exist in schools. Klein and Ortman (1994), Biklen and Pollard (1993) and many other researchers have documented these inequities. What is surprising is that even those teachers who recognize the importance of treating females and minorities fairly do not realize that their actions are most likely to benefit Caucasian male students (Scott & McCollum, 1993). These inequities are bound to have far-reaching effects on student self-concepts.

Some studies have indicated that girls score lower on measures of self-concept than boys. Kelly and Jordan (1990) reported that girls in their study scored lower on scholastic competence and job competence components of self-concept than boys. Similar findings were reported by a 1991 study conducted by the American Association of University Women (AAUW). The AAUW study reported that adolescent boys are more likely than girls to perceive themselves as good enough or smart enough to achieve their career aspirations. However, research by Harper and Purkey (1993) and Stanley (1991b, 1993) reported that female students score higher than male students on self-concept-as-learner. Reasons for the discrepancies in findings probably include (a) the difference in measurement processes; (b) the nature of the research hypotheses; (c) variations in statistical analyses; and (d) differences in populations studied. From conflicting findings, it seems wise to conclude that no real differences exist between female and male students on *mean* self-concept scores. Each student is unique, female or male, and each should be treated as one-of-a-kind.

Research concerning difference between races on self-concept of ability has also produced a mixed bag. Graham (1994) conducted a review of the literature concerning differences in self-concept of ability among white Americans and African-Americans and found little evidence to support the view that African-American students have lower self-concepts of ability. But Harper and Purkey (1993), Stanley (1991b, 1993), and others have reported lower self-concept-as-learner scores for African-American students.

It is not clear what factors interact to affect the reported differences in research findings regarding the variables of gender and race. As indicated earlier in considering gender differences, part of the confusion can be attributed to different measurement instruments, assessment procedures, the varied populations studied, and definitions of terms. Byrne, Shavelson, and Marsh (1992) recommend that future researchers use instruments that give specific self-concept scores, such as self-concept-as-learner or social self-concept.

Regardless of conceptual and methodology confusion about gender and race, continuing inequities exist in schools. As one example of how subtle these inequities can be, a colleague described how he was explaining to a class how to make an inexpensive puppet: "All you need is a ball of cotton, a rubber band, and a white sock . . . " At this moment he looked directly into the eyes of one of his African-American students and realized how unintentionally disinviting his comment was. Whether intentional or unintentional, inequities have no place in the inviting school.

Self-Concept as Guidance System

Dear, dear! How queer everything is today! And yesterday things went on just as usual. I wonder if I've been changed in the night? Let me think: Was I the same when I got up this morning? I almost think I can remember feeling a little different. But if I'm not the same, the next question is "Who in the World am I?" Ah, that's the puzzle!

Alice, Lewis Carroll, *Alice in Wonderland* (1864, 1971, pp. 15–16)

Self-concept is a complex, continuously active system of subjective beliefs about personal existence. It guides behavior and enables each individual to assume particular roles in life. Rather than initiating activity, self-concept serves as a perceptual filter and guides the direction of behavior. A student's self-concept does not *cause* the student to misbehave in the classroom. A better explanation is that the disruptive student has learned to see himself or herself as a troublemaker and behaves accordingly. In other words, self-concept serves as the reference point, or anchoring perception, for behavior. Shavelson and Marsh (1986) refer to self-concept as a "moderator variable." In practical classroom situations, students who have learned to see themselves as "schlemiels" are likely to exhibit "schlemiel" behavior.

Early on, Zimmerman and Allebrand (1965) provided research evidence regarding the guidance function of self-concept. They demonstrated that poor readers lack a sense of personal worth and adequacy to the point where they actively avoid achievement. For poor readers, to study hard and still fail provides unbearable proof of their inadequacy. To avoid such proof and thus suffer less pain, many students deliberately choose not to try. Their defense against failure is secretly to accept themselves as failures! It is better, from the students' viewpoint, not to try than to try and be embarrassed or humiliated. A person with a negative self-concept defends himself or herself against further loss. To understand why this is so, it is important to recognize that from the student's perceptual vantage point any amount of anxiety, no matter how great, appears preferable to other available avenues of behavior.

The determining role of students' beliefs about their self-efficacy has been documented by Schunk (1984, 1989, 1990), Zimmerman, Bandura, and Martinez-Pons (1992) and others. According to self-efficacy researchers, students' positive beliefs in their efficacy for self-regulated learning affected their perceived self-efficacy in school achievement, their academic goal-setting, and their subsequent academic achievement. This analysis suggests that schools should offer experiences that are intentionally designed to strengthen students' self-efficacy beliefs.

Each person acts in accordance with the ways he or she has learned to see himself or herself. From a lifetime of studying his or her own actions and those of significant others, each individual acquires expectations about what things "fit" in his or her personal world. For example, if a new experience is consistent with past experiences already incorporated into the self-concept system, the person easily accepts and assimilates the new experience. If the new experience contradicts those already incorporated, however, the person will probably reject it. Each person incorporates that which is congenial to the self-system already established. Furthermore, actions that are incompatible with the self-image are likely to result in psychological discomfort and anxiety. The result is that everything a person experiences is filtered through, and mediated by, whatever self-concept is already present within the individual. This screening process ensures some consistency within the human personality.

The tendency toward internal consistency appears to be a necessary feature of human personality. It provides the individual's entire being with internal balance, a sense of direction, and a feeling of stability. If individuals adopted new beliefs about themselves rapidly, or if their behaviors were capricious, no integrity would exist in the individual personality and human progress would be difficult to imagine. (Few people would risk flying if they thought the pilots might suddenly perceive themselves as Power Rangers!) Fortunately, most people are remarkably consistent in their self-concepts.

Educators who are not aware of the conservative nature of self-concept are likely to expect quick or miraculous changes in others—such as the teacher who commented, "I'm not going to send another student to the counseling office. I sent a student yesterday. Today he's back and he hasn't changed a bit!" Self-perceptions do change, but not immediately or automatically.

One probable reason for the apparent failure of many school programs designed to enhance, build, or modify students' perceptions of themselves is the tendency to overlook the conservative nature of self-concept. Whether a student's self-perception is psychologically healthy or unhealthy, educationally productive or counterproductive, the student will cling to it the way a drowning person clings to a straw. In fact, students who have learned to see themselves as stupid will experience considerable anxiety over their own successful performance. Students who have learned to expect failure are even likely to sabotage their own efforts when they meet unexpected success. They actively maintain their self-pictures even if the pictures are false and unhealthy.

One additional point relates to the consistency of self-concept: Being correct in one's assumptions about oneself has reward value, even if the assumption is negative. A student may take a certain pleasure in thinking, "See, just as I thought, I knew nobody in this lousy school cares whether I live or die!" Being right, even about negative feelings toward oneself, can be satisfying. This is one reason why one-shot attempts, quick-fix efforts, or programs that lack consistency in philosophy and dependability in direction are often unsuccessful and may even incur student resistance or anger.

Although self-concepts tend toward consistency, changes in self-concepts are possible. New ideas filter into the self-concept throughout life while some old ideas fade away. This continuous process creates flexibility in human personality and allows psychological development. The hypothetical reason for the assimilation of new ideas and the expulsion of old ones is that each person has a basic need to maintain, protect, and enhance the self-concept—to obtain positive self-regard as well as positive regard from others. This basic human characteristic is a tremendous given for the classroom teacher. Rather than struggling to motivate students, the teacher may assume that students are *always* motivated. Thus, the teacher can concentrate his or her energies toward influencing the direction this motivation will take. The student's motor is already running. Education's function is to place the signs, build the roads, direct the traffic, and teach good driving—but not to drive the car.

It will be helpful at this point to consider the nature of motivation. From a perceptual point of view (Avila & Purkey, 1966), there is only one kind of motivation—an internal and continuous incentive that every individual has at all times, in all places, during any activity. As Combs (1962) explained: "People are always motivated; in fact, they are never unmotivated. They may not be motivated to do what we would prefer they do, but it can never be truly said that they are unmotivated" (p. 85). This view of motivation should be tremendously reassuring to teachers, for it assumes motivation is a force that comes from within the student. Rather than spending energy trying to motivate students, teachers can use their talents to invite students to explore the world of knowledge and imaginative possibilities. These invitations to learning are most likely to be accepted and acted upon when students see them as contributing to their own positive self-regard.

Significance of Positive Self-Regard

A person who doubts himself is like a man who would enlist in the ranks of his enemies and bear arms against himself. He makes his failure certain by himself being the first person to be convinced of it.

Alexandre Dumas, *The Three Musketeers* (1844/1962)

To learn in school, students require sufficient confidence in themselves and their abilities to make some effort to succeed. Self-regard and efforts to control one's destiny correlate highly. As Thomas Szasz (1976) explained, "The more self-esteem a person has, the greater as a rule, is his desire, and his ability, to control himself" (p. 57). Without self-confidence, students easily succumb to apathy, dependency, and loss of self-control. Too often, the real problem of negative self-esteem is hidden beneath such labels as *unmotivated, undisciplined, unable,* or *uninterested.* The classroom result is that students with low self-regard will expect the worst in every situation and will be constantly afraid of saying the wrong word or doing the wrong thing.

The importance of self-efficacy and self-regard has been documented by Coopersmith's study of the antecedents of self-esteem among children. Coopersmith (1967) reported: "There are pervasive and significant differences in the experiential worlds and social behaviors of persons who differ in self-esteem. Persons high in their own self-estimation approach tasks and persons with the expectation that they will be well-received and successful" (p. 70). Similar findings of other researchers (Rosenberg, 1979; Tesser & Campbell, 1983; Covington, 1984; Chapman, 1988; Hattie, 1992) show that individuals high in self-esteem are more independent of external reinforcement and more consistent in their social behavior.

Research also provides evidence that people with negative self-regard tend to be more destructive, more anxious, more stressed, and more likely to manifest psychosomatic symptoms than people of average or high self-regard. Although feeling worthless is not the same as being worthless, the impact on student behavior is often the same. "I never raise my hand in class," a high-school student wrote. "I guess it goes back to elementary school; when I asked my teacher about a question, she responded, 'Oh, that's the easiest problem in the chapter; any dummy could figure that out.'" Whether intentional or unintentional, a disinviting comment can have lasting and devastating results on self-esteem.

From an invitational perspective, one of the most damaging things a teacher can teach a child is not to try. Even if something does not work, the student has learned something. Perhaps the only real failure in life is to fail to try.

What research findings and student reports on the importance of self-regard mean for educators is that many common classroom problems such as student disruption, inattention, apathy, and anxiety probably indicate negative self-regard by the students exhibiting such behavior.

Research on classroom discipline (Branch, Damico & Purkey, 1977) reveals a significant relationship between students' low self-concepts as learners and their misbehavior in the classroom. Branch, Damico, and Purkey (1977) evaluated disruptive and nondisruptive middle-school students (grades five through eight) on their professed and inferred academic self-concepts. Analysis revealed significant differences between the two groups. Those students identified by their behavior as disruptive had significantly lower self-concepts as learners than did students identified as nondisruptive. The study's theoretical implication was that students' negative feelings about themselves as learners may be a contributing factor in student disruption. Related research in juvenile delinquency has indicated a strong relationship between negative self-concept and delinquency. Self-concept may eventually prove to be a significant mediating variable that will help educators understand many types of seemingly unrelated behavior problems.

Compounding the problem of negative self-regard is the apparent correlation between a person's self-regard and the degree to which he or she is disturbed by the poor opinion of others. Students are highly sensitive to the behavior of others toward them, and their feelings can remain injured for many years, creating a downward spiraling effect on self-regard.

One teacher revealed the long-term impact of real or imagined slights thusly:

Several years ago a young man, now the assistant manager of a large grocery store, stopped me at the counter and said: "You don't remember me, do you?" I replied that I remembered his face and that he had been a student of mine. Since at least ten years had passed, I could not remember his name. His remark that followed stunned me. I did not try to argue or insist that I had never said it. Instead I said: "I only hope that I never said such a thing to you or to any other student. I hope you are doing well." I walked away, wondering if I were guilty, if I had—in disgust, anger, or frustration—said it. I made a commitment never to let it happen again. This is what the assistant manager told me I said to him: "Right before I quit school, you told me that I'd never amount to anything. You see. I've proved you wrong."

Behavior is guided by self-concept; whether real or imagined, a teacher's disinviting message has the potential to take on its own life and exist for many years, particularly in the minds of students already unsure of their own worth and ability. As House (1992) demonstrated, academic self-concept is continuously modified on the basis of perceived school experiences.

Efforts to Promote Positive Self-Regard

Beane (1991) analyzed ways that schools can work to encourage positive and realistic self concepts in students. According to Beane, there are solid reasons why schools should be concerned with how students feel about themselves. In his view, "It is a moral imperative for schools, especially in a time when other social institutions and agencies seem unwilling or unable to provide support and encouragement in the process of growing up" (p. 250). He argues that efforts to cultivate positive self-regard in students is a way to eventually address social concerns like racism, sexism, poverty, and homelessness.

Beane sees three general approaches to improving student self-concept. One approach involves such activities as sensitivity training. For example, students might sit in a circle for 15 minutes one day a week and talk about how much they like themselves. A second approach involves introducing self-concept courses or programs that are taught during the school day. This would include commercially or locally prepared instruction units built around self-esteem exercises. Beane reports there may be more than 350 self-esteem building programs now in existence, with approximately 30 programs used nationally. Unfortunately, little in the research literature documents the value of packaged programs in promoting positive and realistic student self-concepts.

A third approach to addressing self-concept, the one advocated by Beane, is to consider the importance of the total school environment as an ecological system in which positive and realistic self-concepts can be fostered. This is clearly the approach of invitational education because perceptions and self-concepts do not develop in isolation—they are the products of social like. Social living is strongly shaped by guiding ideals.

Democratic Practice

A democracy is more than a form of government;
it is primarily a mode of associated living, of conjoint
communicated experiences.

John Dewey, *Democracy and Education* **(1916, p. 87)**

The third foundation of invitational education is democratic practice. Democracy is not some final, easily agreed upon political concept (Gutmann, 1987), nor a strict set of formal governmental procedures (Stuhr, 1993). Rather, democratic practice is a guiding ideal that focuses on developing continuous dialogue and mutual respect among people regarding shared aspects of their lives.

Dewey emphasized the critical importance of communication in *Democracy and Education* (1916). For Dewey, it is through the communication process that people can develop and maintain common values and enjoy community living. Mutual respect is a hallmark of this commitment to a life of dialogue.

Democratic practice is founded on open and free dialogue which promotes social responsibility. As people communicate in a pluralistic society, they have to deal with an endless variety of individual perceptual worlds, self-concepts, and cultural perspectives. This requires social intelligence, which is the ability to use a variety of perspectives, to view things from the viewpoint of others, and to deal with the complexities of democratic living. The development of social intelligence leads to a stronger sense of collective responsibility—a sense that all are in it together.

As a guiding ideal, democratic practice points to ever-enriching communicative process. As an ideal, democratic practice should not be judged useless because it is not attained in every instance. Rather, ideals, as Robert Nozick (1989) indicated, should by judged on the basis of whether they enable people to attain more of what they consider to be of worth. A commitment to democratic practice is therefore a commitment to the conditions and processes that make mutual respect and continuous dialogue possible. These are essential to invitational education.

Summary

This chapter explored the three foundations of invitational education: the perceptual tradition, self-concept theory, and democratic practice. The perceptual tradition was described as a focus on the individual's world of experience, the learning of personal reality, and the ability to reflect upon perceptions and imagine the future. Self-concept theory was presented to show how a person's perceived self develops primarily from inviting or disinviting messages sent, received, interpreted, and acted upon. Each person has a strong tendency to protect his or her self-concept against conflicting pressures, to think as well of oneself as circumstances permit, and to want to be regarded positively by significant others. Democratic practice was shown to be the guiding ideal that points to ever-enriching communicative processes—processes that promote the development of all in a pluralistic society. Chapter Three examines the stance necessary to maintain an inviting perspective and sets the stage for the development of skills and the handling of challenging situations presented in Chapters Four and Five.

3

The Inviting Approach

And now here is my secret, a very simple secret:
It is only with the heart that one can see rightly.
What is essential is invisible to the eye.

Antoine de Saint-Exupéry, *The Little Prince* (1943, p. 87)

To be optimally inviting to oneself and others, educators require an understanding of the perceptual tradition and self-concept theory and need to apply this understanding in actual situations involving real people. This involves the artful blending of *teacher perceptions, teacher stance,* and *teacher behavior* into a working theory of practice.

Teacher Perceptions

Teachers who have been in classrooms for any length of time know that teaching is a fragile, sometimes puzzling, process. Things can go well when least expected, whereas the best-prepared lesson can fail. Why a class succeeds or fails is likely to be found in the teacher. As explained in Chapter Two, people behave according to the particular beliefs they hold about themselves, others, and the world. Teachers who believe that students are able, valuable, and responsible are well on their way to becoming the sort of teacher advocated in this book.

No single explanation can cover the complexity of the educative process. It is increasingly evident, however, that the teacher's perceptions of students, as reflected in his or her behavior, have the power to influence how students view themselves and how well they learn in school. As Jourard (1968) explained: "The teacher who turns on the dull student, the coach who elicits a magnificent performance from someone of whom it could not be expected, are people who themselves have an image of the pupils' possibilities; and they were effective in realizing their images" (p.126). Like a sculptor who envisions something in a block of marble that others cannot see, the inviting teacher perceives possibilities in students that others miss.

Studies that have focused most directly on the perceptions of professional helpers include those of Combs, Avila, and Purkey (1978); Combs, Soper, Gooding, Benton, Dickman, and Usher (1969); O'Roark (1974); Wasicsko (1977); Bandura (1986); Bingham, Haubrich, White, and Zipp (1990); and Kagan (1992).

Combs's research studies spanned more than a decade, and he and his associates investigated how successful teachers and other professional helpers organize their perceptions of themselves, others, and the world. The research also investigated how these perceptual organizations influence effectiveness in helping others.

Combs reported that effective helpers in many professions—including teaching, counseling, nursing, the ministry, and public service—can be distinguished from less effective helpers on the basis of their perceptions. He concluded that a high degree of similarity exists among the belief systems of "good helpers" in numerous professional fields. Good teachers, for example, may be clearly identified from poor ones on the basis of their perceptions of people as able rather than unable, friendly rather than unfriendly, worthy rather than unworthy, dependable rather than undependable, helpful rather than hindering, and internally, rather than externally, motivated (Combs et al., 1969).

More recently, researchers have focused on educators' belief systems to understand how they function as professionals (Clark, 1988; Cole, 1989; Fenstermacher, 1986; Nespor, 1987; Pintrich, 1990; Weinstein,

1989; Wilson, 1990). According to M. Frank Pajares (1992), the belief systems of educators should be a major focus for educational research and practice. These and other studies imply that how teachers and other helpers perceive students heavily influences their success or failure in teaching.

Growing evidence supports two important assumptions of invitational education. First, inviting and disinviting messages primarily result from perceptions. Second, these messages significantly affect students' self-concepts as well as their attitudes toward school, the relationships they form in school, and their school achievement. Emerging research continues to support the concept that boys and girls are more committed to academic learning when they are surrounded by a caring and supportive school environment (Eccles & Midgley 1989; Matthews, 1991).

Clearly, educators should work on developing their positive perceptions of themselves, others, and education if they wish to be a beneficial presence in students' lives. Positive perceptions means viewing students as able, valuable, and responsible as well as seeing oneself and education in essentially favorable ways. These teacher perceptions are worth considering in greater detail.

Viewing Students As Able

Where I come from, we have great universities. When students graduate, they have two things you need. A diploma and a degree. There, then, is your diploma—" He handed the scarecrow a rolled up parchment— "and your degree. You are now a Th.D.—Doctor of Thinkology!" The scarecrow took the diploma, and frowned. Then he looked up and smiled a huge smile! "Gosh!" he cried, "I think I can think!"

The Wizard of Oz. **From the Metro-Goldwyn-Mayer film, 1939. Original story by L. Frank Baum. Adapted by Horace J. Elias.**

As presented in Chapter One, an important assumption of invitational education is that each student has relatively untapped capabilities for thinking, choosing, and learning and that these capabilities can be realized in an optimally inviting school environment. This assumption is supported by what is known about the capabilities of children.

From birth, infants are marvelously curious, seeming to obtain a sense of pleasure and satisfaction from understanding and mastering their environments. From a very young age, children rapidly acquire knowledge, which they apply to gain further understanding of their environments.

Today educators recognize that children possess far greater capacities for learning than almost anyone previously had thought possible. Human intelligence is currently recognized as a dynamic potential, rather than a static entity. Simply defined, intelligence is the level of mental functioning that is reflected in the quality or effectiveness of an individual's behavior. This mental functioning level can be strongly influenced by either facilitating or debilitating environments. Research (Bloom, 1976; Matthews, 1991) has documented that most students develop a desire for further learning when they are provided with favorable learning conditions.

In concluding his classic study on the relationship between intelligence and experience, J. McVickors Hunt (1961) commented: "It is highly unlikely that any society has developed a system of child rearing and education that maximizes the potential of the individuals which compose it. Probably no individual has ever lived whose full potential for happy intellectual interest and growth has been achieved" (p. 346). In other words, human potential, although not always apparent, is always there, waiting to be discovered and invited forth.

Throughout their school years, some students become more creative, some less so; some become excited about learning, some become bored and disillusioned; some become intellectually active, some less active. Some students fall in love with books, others learn to hate them. Some develop a passion for physical exercise, others learn to avoid it. The entire process is heavily influenced by the belief systems of teachers as manifested in their actions (Goodman, 1988; Calderhead & Robson, 1991).

In addition to their actual classroom presence, students exist as mental images in teachers' minds. Teachers who believe that certain children cannot learn or benefit from instruction will have little success in teaching them. As John Childs (1931) emphasized more than a half-century ago, if educators believe that half the people cannot think for themselves, they will establish a school system that will actually make it impossible for half of the people to think for themselves.

Happily, when teachers have positive views of students' abilities, students are likely to respond in positive ways. This process has been documented by Good (1981); Good, Biddle, and Brophy (1975); Good and Brophy (1978); Insel and Jacobson (1975); Jones and Panitch (1971); Pajares (1992); Pintrich (1990); and others. It was also documented by a student who wrote, "I am 21 and a painting major. When I was in the sixth grade I suggested a mural design for our school. My teacher was so pleased she ordered the paint, ladder, even excused me from regular class so I could complete the mural. I usually tire of my past work, or don't think it's very good, yet I still believe that mural was one of the best paintings I've ever done. I think it turned out so well because the teacher had such faith in my ability." Students develop best when they share the company of teachers who see them as possessing relatively untapped abilities in myriad areas and who invite them to realize their potential.

Perceiving Students as Valuable

Teacher: "Would you like me to refer to you as Black or Afro-American?"

Student: "I think I would like to be referred to as Joanne."

When professional helpers believe that each student or client is a person of value, their behavior will reflect this belief (Robertiello & Schoenewolf, 1987). People constantly communicate their real feelings in the silent language, the language of behavior. When teachers perceive their students positively, they are more likely to involve themselves with their students, both personally and professionally, and a *doing-with* as opposed to a *doing-to* process often results. The warmth of this teacher-student partnership is illustrated by a middle-school student who wrote, "Mr. Russell is my best teacher, and he asked me to remind him to watch his weight— and I do, too!" Education is, or should be, a cooperative enterprise. An atmosphere of mutual respect and positive regard increases the likelihood of cooperation and student success in school. This atmosphere is particularly important in working with students identified as disadvantaged.

According to Graham's research (1994), the most effective teachers of disadvantaged or minority group students are those who stress the unique value of the individual student. Such teachers are sensitive to the fact that children show uneven patterns of achievement and that standardized test scores for groups of children do not necessarily indicate a particular child's general mental ability. These teachers understand that student comparisons can be perceived as very disinviting, particularly for those who are told again and again, both verbally and nonverbally, that they are *less* able, *less* valuable, and *less* responsible than their more advantaged peers (Markus & Wurf, 1987).

Unfortunately, positive attitudes toward disadvantaged students seem to be in short supply in some schools. Research indicates that many teachers hold lower expectations for the performance of disadvantaged students (McAdoo & McAdoo, 1985); are likely to behave differently and inappropriately toward these students, by refusing them sufficient time to answer questions or rewarding them for inappropriate behavior (Good, 1980; Good & Brophy, 1977); and tend to provide them with fewer verbal and nonverbal reinforcements (Friedman & Friedman, 1973). The unfortunate result is that African-American students are over-represented in the ranks of those who fail in school and are five times more likely to drop out of high school (Edelman, 1985). These and other findings indicate that it is vital that educators develop and maintain a positive view of all students.

One additional reason for seeing students as valuable is that such a view may contribute significantly to their mental health. As early as 1947, Erich Fromm pointed out that feelings of worthlessness characterize a suffering personality. Similar conclusions were presented by Clark Moustakas (1966). Listing ways in which educators contribute to the development of self-esteem, Moustakas first listed the importance of confirming the student as being of noncomparable and nonmeasureable worth. Teachers signal their positive beliefs in countless ways. One student wrote, "My third-grade teacher . . . I was new in the school (in the middle of the year) and was lonely, shy, alone. It was a cold, winter day and I had a cold. I sneezed very hard and didn't have a tissue. I tried to hide it in my hand, in a fist. Mrs. Benedict very tactfully brought me a tissue and slipped it in my hand. I was very thankful." When teachers believe in each student's value, they telegraph this belief in everything they do and every way they do it.

Seeing Students as Responsible

Human beings are not born once and for all on the day their mothers give birth to them, . . . life obliges them over and over again to give birth to themselves.

Gabriel García Marquez, *Love in the Time of Cholera* (1988, p. 165)

In North American schools today, the number of things a student can be ordered or coerced to do is, or should be, kept to a minimum. Both student desire and performance tend to deteriorate when external constraints, such as threats, surveillance, punishments, and bribes, are accentuated (Clifford, 1990). According to various researchers (Deci & Ryan, 1987; Kruglanski, Stein & Riter, 1977; Lepper & Hodell, 1989; Matthews, 1991), feelings of self-control and personal responsibility elicit more creative thinking in children and encourage greater cognitive flexibility and persistence.

From an inviting perspective, a teacher cannot "learn" a student. Students choose to learn, just as they choose *not* to learn in the face of ridicule, embarrassment, or coercion. Invitational education builds on the assumption that students will elect to learn those things they perceive to be significant in their personal lives. What teachers can do, therefore, is conduct themselves and their classes so that students are consistently summoned to perceive the significance of course content, to choose meaningful programs, to cooperate in the learning process, and to participate actively in school activities.

Teachers who recognize the definite limits of their powers to make students learn are in a good position to try alternative ways of teaching. These teachers can more easily find their own best ways of inviting students to discover the personal pleasure of self-directed learning. For example, a Minnesota high-school science teacher was so successful at inviting students to learn science that some students continued to attend his class even after dropping out of school! One such "drop-in" en route to this science class was intercepted by a secretary, who demanded to know why this drop-out was in the building. The science teacher, overhearing the question, quietly took the secretary aside and said, "Our job is not to ask students why they're here; our job is to ask them why they're *not* here." Several days later, the principal asked another of the teacher's drop-ins why he continued to attend class. The boy responded, "Frankly, I just want to see what he's gonna do next!"

By respecting students and believing in their ability, value, and self-directing powers, teachers can spend less time trying to force students to learn and more energy developing an exciting and appealing environment for learning to occur. During a presentation to a large audience, Leo Buscaglia offered a beautiful analogy of how this might be accomplished. Buscaglia used the metaphor of knowledge being a marvelous feast. What the teacher can do is prepare food with great relish and care, sample it frequently, dance around the table at mealtime, and invite students to join the celebration! This approach seems to make better sense than trying to force-feed unwilling students—and is certainly more gratifying.

Available research (Good & Brophy, 1994; Lepper & Greene, 1975; Lepper & Hodell, 1989; Maehr, 1974; Mahoney, 1974; Matthews, 1991) supports the idea that choice and feelings of personal responsibility promote school achievement. The apparent rule is that when students are given meaningful choices in their education they are likely to learn more, for they are learning what they have elected to learn.

The importance of personal choice is also evident in areas other than education. As early as 1960, Lippitt and White demonstrated through experimentally controlled social climates the value of leaders who encouraged self-direction in workers. This finding has been supported by research by Ouchi (1981), and Wirth (1983, 1992) indicating the importance of workers' feelings of autonomy in their work activities. Feelings of being responsible result from a vast array of possible modes of thought. People tend to value what they do when they believe they have some choice in doing it and when they sense value in doing it. Csikszentmihalyi (1990) maintains that feelings of responsibility are connected to some activity that is goal-oriented and that is related to some social or contributive purpose. Thus, self-concept is linked to effort and achievement.

Finally, a belief in people's ability to make intelligent choices is the foundation of a democratic way of life. When Thomas Jefferson wrote the Declaration of Independence, he never wavered in his faith that people, when free to choose, will find their own best ways. He believed that if individuals were unable to handle freedom of choice, the remedy was not to take it away from them but to inform them by education. Similarly, Dewey proclaimed throughout his career that the best cure for the problems of democracy is more democracy. When students are encouraged to make significant choices in their lives, they are far more likely, later in life, to maintain personal integrity in the face of external pressure and manipulation. They are also more likely to support a democratic philosophy of government.

Educators can better facilitate student responsibility when they hold certain perceptions about themselves. Self-confidence, self efficacy, and positive self-regard are associated with success as a professional helper.

Viewing Oneself Positively

I to myself am dearer than a friend.

William Shakespeare, *Two Gentlemen of Verona* Act 11, Scene vi

Perceiving students as able, valuable, and responsible is much easier when educators have a positive and realistic view of themselves. A growing body of literature in the education, psychology, and counseling fields centers on the assumption that when teachers better understand, accept, and like themselves, they have a much greater capacity to understand, accept, and like students. A positive, realistic view of oneself is an important ingredient in behaving in an inviting manner. "Mrs. Reynolds expected good things of us," a high-school student wrote, "and we could tell she also expected good things of herself."

The ability to speak to oneself about oneself in positive, realistic ways is an important aspect of invitational education. Positive self-talk has been associated with the effectiveness of professional helpers (Fugua, Newman, Anderson & Johnson, 1986; Stanley, 1991a). To understand this, imagine two science teachers. Both possess essentially the same knowledge and skills. During each teacher's class, two students carry on a private conversation, ignoring the carefully prepared demonstration by the teacher. This student behavior elicits different *internal dialogues* (what we say to ourselves about ourselves, sometimes called *self-talk*) from the two teachers. The first teacher thinks, "I've stayed up half the night to prepare this demonstration, and those two students are not paying a bit of attention to me. I know I'm not the greatest teacher, but why do kids have to be so rude?" The second teacher, faced with exactly the same student behavior, is more positive and realistic and thinks something like this: "Those two students are not paying attention. That's too bad, because this is an important and well-prepared demonstration. I'll try to find additional ways to make these demonstrations more interesting. Meanwhile, after class I'll talk to these students about the reasons for their lack of attention."

The first teacher's perception and internal dialogue are self-defeating. They exaggerate the meaning of the student's behavior, they emphasize the two students' lack of attention over the attention of all the other students in the class, and they overgeneralize the situation by assuming personal inadequacy. Clearly, the first teacher's internal dialogue is inappropriate, anxiety-producing, and self-defeating. The second teacher makes a more positive appraisal of the classroom situation and forms a more realistic and constructive pattern of internal self-statements.

Awareness of one's internal dialogue and realistic appraisals of classroom experiences have been stressed by numerous researchers who report that what people say internally about themselves plays an important role in their adaptive or maladaptive behavior (Kendall, Howard & Hays, 1989; Meichenbaum, 1977, 1985; Thomas, 1982). Teachers are too often overly critical in what they say to themselves about themselves. "The worst enemies of teachers," as one teacher noted, "are teachers!" An important way to become more personally and professionally inviting is to be gentle with yourself, to be aware of self-defeating perceptions, and to practice positive and productive self-statements.

Perceiving yourself positively also means applying the categories *able, valuable,* and *responsible* to your own existence. The perception that people are worthy of inviting, that they have relatively untapped potential, and that they can make meaningful choices in their lives applies to oneself as well as to others. Positive and realistic perceptions of the self are essential parts of the inviting approach to education. The same is true regarding positive perceptions of education.

Perceiving Education Affirmatively

The result of the educative process is capacity for further education.

John Dewey, *Democracy and Education* (1916, p. 79)

Teaching is a delicate relationship between and among people aiming at a positive enduring attitude to learning (Schrag, 1995). Teaching involves knowing something worth knowing and desiring to share and extend this knowledge with others. Educators who are personally and professionally inviting not only have positive perceptions about themselves and others, they also have rich and extensive perceptions about the subjects they desire to teach. One student said, "Because Mr. Chambers opened up so many doors of knowledge to us, I felt smarter and eager to learn."

An example of a powerful summons to learning is found in *The Once and Future King*, where Merlin is talking to Wart (the future King Arthur):

"The best thing for being sad," replied Merlin, beginning to puff and blow, "is to learn something. That is the only thing that never fails. You may grow old and trembling in your anatomies, you may lie awake at night listening to the disorder of your veins, you may miss your only love, you may see the world about you devastated by evil lunatics, or know your honor trampled in the sewers of baser minds. There is only one thing for it then—to learn. Learn why the world wags and what wags it. That is the only thing which the mind can never exhaust, never alienate, never be tortured by, never fear or distrust, and never dream of regretting. Learning is the thing for you" (White, 1958, pp. 185–186).

Involved in the process of extending invitations to learning is the teacher's personal relationship to the content and essence of what he or she teaches. A teacher who can perceive meaning, clarity, significance, and excitement in what he or she teaches is better able to invite students to do likewise. In addition, the likelihood of an invitation to learning being accepted increases when the teacher is perceived as having expertise, enthusiasm, and sound judgment, as well as being seen as caring and trustworthy. These events are most likely to emerge when the teacher develops and maintains a certain stance that serves as a basis for subsequent action.

Teacher Stance

Invitational education is a theory of practice; that is it is about putting perceptions to work. To exist, invitations must be sent and received; they cannot merely be wished for. People do not reach their potential because others simply wish them well. Thus, invitational education practitioners exhibit a consistent behavioral framework. The term "teacher stance" is useful here to indicate the general position from which one operates and one's typical pattern of action.

In baseball, a stance is the unique way a batter digs in to make solid contact with the ball. Although no one stance is perfect, there are some basic mechanics. Players must develop a stance that is sound, comfortable, and deserving of their confidence in order to focus their attention on efforts to make the right connection. Likewise, a teacher's stance involves uniqueness, personal ownership, and functional criteria. The stance focuses a teacher's perceptions so the teacher can make solid contact. Although it cannot guarantee success, a good stance makes it more likely that beneficial things will happen. The use of stance here is similar to the concept "teacher perspectives," developed by Janesick (1977) and enriched by Tabachnick and Zeichner (1984), Clark and Peterson (1986), and Pajares (1992). Stance goes beyond beliefs in that it is action-oriented and gives life to goals, purposes, and attitudes. In invitational education, a teacher's good stance is built around four assumptions: trust, respect, optimism, and intentionality.

Trust

Trust is indispensable to the inviting process. Invitational education is most likely to thrive in an atmosphere of trust. Teachers who wish to become more personally and professionally inviting develop this trusting atmosphere by believing in themselves and consistently behaving in a positive and dependable manner. This involves maintaining a warm, caring relationship with students, one in which teachers can be "real" with themselves and others.

Invitational education is a cooperative, collaborative activity in which process is an equal partner to product. Support for this assumption is provided by Bergman and Gaitskill (1990), who reported that students ranked teachers' trustworthy relationships with students first, even above professional competence. This finding was also reported by Amos (1985), who found that students ranked teacher "consideration" above such qualities as "competency" and "commitment," and by Galbo (1989) who reported that teachers who developed personal relationships with students had the most significant influence on them.

In professions other than education, trust is viewed as a critical variable in relationships. Ouchi (1981) developed a model for successful management ("Theory Z") that emphasized the values of consensual decision-making. Theory Z was the forerunner of such popular innovations as "teacher empowerment," "outcome based education," "quality circles," and "site-based management."

Within education, trust is established and maintained through sources identified by Arceneaux (1994). These sources include, but are not restricted to, *reliability* (consistency, dependability, and predictability), *genuineness* (authenticity and congruence), *truthfulness* (honesty, correctness of opinion, and validity of assertion), and *competence* (intelligent behavior, expertness, and knowledge). The teacher, by being reliable, genuine, truthful, and competent, inspires trust in students and colleagues. Without trust, it is unlikely that anything of positive significance will occur in classrooms or schools.

Respect

A second important aspect of a teacher's stance deals with respect. Nothing in invitational education is more important than respect for people.

The importance of respect is underscored by research. In study after study (Amos, 1985; Lambeth, 1980; Ripley, 1985; Smith, 1987; Turner, 1983), involving more than 2,000 secondary and postsecondary students, a consistently high correlation was reported among indicators of invitational teaching (trust, respect, optimism, and intentionality) and positive student outcomes.

Arnold and Roach (1989), in their study of teachers' nonverbal behaviors, reported that teachers who demonstrated respect for students through such simple processes as starting and ending class on time tended to have students who viewed the class as important and therefore tended to study more. Goffin (1989) offered a series of practical suggestions on ways that teacher can demonstrate respect for students. She suggested that teachers should develop an appreciation for each student's uniqueness. Central to this teacher perspective is an appreciation for cultural differences and valuing the rich complexity of each human being. This agrees with the thinking of Dewey (1930) who pointed out in *Individualism Old and New* that being a unique member of a meaningful group is important for both the individual and the group. In fact, Dewey felt that the more democratic a group is, the more the group experience builds on the unique perspectives and interests of its members, and thus the more the group experience becomes a source of educational development for all involved.

As an example, one of the authors had the pleasure of watching a military unit from the United States Army present a drill. As the units performed, the observer could spot African war dances, British precision drill, American Indian movements, Japanese Bushito, and assorted other influences. The artful integration of many traditions was spectacular.

Respect in the school means that whatever a classroom should be, it should not be a place where people are embarrassed, insulted, humiliated, or subjected to prejudice. If there are policies, practices, programs, or whatever that cannot be performed in accordance with respect, or if there are faculty, administrators, or staff who cannot or will not function in a consistently respectful manner, they should not be in schools. Demeaning practices such as public ridicule, invidious comparisons, unicultural thinking, autocratic processes, deliberate humiliation, sexual, racial, or homophobic reactions, and corporal punishment cannot exist in a school that considers itself inviting.

Optimism

Optimists do better in school, succeed more at life tasks, and even age better and live longer (Seligman, 1990). By working to develop an optimistic perspective, educators are on the path to a good and successful life. This optimism involves both self and others.

Invitational education presents a positive vision of human existence: that individuals are valuable, able, capable of self-direction and should be treated accordingly. This starkly contrasts with those who find value in pessimism and cynicism. What educator has not heard the doomsday reports of those coworkers who arrive at schools with such cynical comments as:

"What can you expect from people like that?"

"They don't want to learn."

"They just want to cause trouble."

"Well, you know how they are."

"They have no motivation."

"They take no pride."

"They simply don't have the ability."

"They just don't care."

Educators create the facts that make their hypotheses come true. If the teacher believes that students don't want to learn, do want to cause trouble, are unmotivated, and don't care, then their students will live *down* to their teacher's expectations. Research (Harter, 1988; Matthews, 1991) points out that the more students sense positive regard from significant others, the more they feel valued and the harder they are likely to work.

Good and Brophy (1994) reported that teachers tend to treat low and high achievers differently based on their optimistic or pessimistic views regarding these students' likelihood of success. Teachers give low achievers less time to answer a question and more often criticize low achievers for failure. Teachers tend to give high achievers more eye contact and are more friendly, smile more, and give more nonverbal signals of support to perceived high achievers. All these behaviors reflect optimism or pessimism.

Intentionality

By definition, an invitation is a purposive act. It is intended to offer something beneficial for consideration. This definition suggests a purposive act intended to benefit the recipient.

The more intentionality the teacher can exhibit, the more accurate his or her judgments and the more decisive his or her behavior. An extreme example of intentionality is illustrated by a Hollywood agent who was told to get lost and "not come back for ten years." The agent responded: "Morning or afternoon?"

Another aspect of intentionality is that it helps teachers generate multiple choices in a given situation. Ivey (1977) demonstrated that intentional individuals can develop plans, act on many possible opportunities, and evaluate the effect of these actions. As proposed by Schmidt, (1984; 1994) and others, it takes intentionality to be inviting, particularly when facing obstacles, challenges, and apparent rejection.

The value of intentionality is revealed in one student's successful change in behavior, as described by Purkey and Strahan (1986):

Keith was one of those students "whose reputation preceded him" to the middle school. His elementary teachers passed along horror stories of his escapades; the day he inked his hands to leave a trail of blue prints along the white walls of his third grade classroom, the time in fourth grade when he used his scissors to "trim" the hair of a girl seated in front of him, his record number of trips to the principal's office in fifth grade. According to records, his previous teachers had tried everything from conferring, consulting and confronting, to detention, demerits, and deterrents—all to no avail.

When the sixth grade teacher learned that Keith would be one of his students in the fall, he began to plan for success. Several weeks before the start of the school year he sent a card to all his incoming students (including a special note to Keith) welcoming them to his class. Next, he studied Keith's records and found not only an abundance of referrals but also a number of indications of academic potential.

On the first day of class, students were asked to complete autobiographical inventories describing their interests. Keith listed "pets" and "reading" among his likes. When Keith interrupted class discussion with, "Hey, did you hear about the guy who tried to dry his hat in the microwave?," the teacher waved off his comment and moved closer to him. A second disruption was greeted by the teacher with "We will talk about this after class."

*During the private conference the teacher explained his
expectations for the class and asked Keith to talk about his
expectations as well. During the conference the teacher also asked
Keith to help him set up a class aquarium. After the aquarium was
operating, the teacher encouraged Keith to join several students as
tutors in a reading program for younger students. Maintaining the
aquarium and serving as a tutor helped Keith feel a part of the class
and assisted him in improving his behavior. Keith acted up from
time to time, but the teacher's intentional efforts were successful in
improving the student's behavior.*

In the situation with Keith, invitational teaching is visible. The
teacher worked to develop a relationship based on mutual trust and
respect. The teacher was optimistic that Keith could learn self-discipline
and was intentional with a plan of action. At its best, invitational teaching
can overcome years of unruly student behavior. Chapter Five will present
ways to maintain an inviting stance in the face of major obstacles,
challenges, and apparent rejection.

Teacher Behaviors

Earlier the idea was presented that each professional has the ability and
responsibility to function in a professionally inviting manner. However, it
is possible for a message, no matter how well-meaning, to be perceived as
disinviting. Attractive or repellent qualities remain in the eyes of the
beholder. There is no guarantee that the most well-intentioned actions
will be viewed positively by others.

Numerous classification systems have been developed for categoriz-
ing messages. The classification system that fits the approach presented
in this book involves the following four categories: *Level One*, intentionally disinviting; *Level Two*, unintentionally disinviting; *Level Three*,
unintentionally inviting; and *Level Four*, intentionally inviting.

Level One: Intentionally Disinviting

Acknowledging that some messages are meant to be disinviting is painful.
Comments such as "Shut up" or "You never use your head" fit into this
level. Professionals functioning at the intentionally disinviting level are

aware of the disabling, demeaning, and devaluing potential of their behavior. Exactly why some few people choose to function at this bottom level is unclear. But regardless of the reasons—whether because of racial or gender prejudice, unrequited love, personal inadequacy, or negative self-image—if they are unable or unwilling to change, fellow professionals have the responsibility to caringly but firmly remove them from daily contact with students.

Fortunately, relatively few educators function at *Level One* for any extended period of time. Intentionally disinviting messages are usually communicated in fits of anger or frustration. Here is an extreme example provided by a student:

> When I was in kindergarten, Mrs. Hall made me sit beside Ilmar. No one wanted to sit next to him because he smelled bad and always had a runny nose. One day he bit me on the arm. I told Mrs. Hall and she said if he did it again he would have to move. So JoLynn (my friend) said she would bite my arm (teeth marks for proof) and I could tell Mrs. Hall. When I showed Mrs. Hall my arm she became furious. She asked me if I wanted to bite Ilmar back. Of course I didn't, so she bit him on the arm.

A major problem with *Level One* behavior is that these intentionally disinviting actions tend to be justified by some individuals as being "good" for students. The authors of this book can think of no circumstances in which it is good to demean students or where a professional can justify intentionally disinviting behavior.

Another form of intentionally disinviting behavior is exhibited by the person who sends mixed, but predominantly disinviting messages. People who behave this way mean to be disinviting, but may alter their behavior when confronted. For example, in the movie *On Golden Pond*, Norman (Henry Fonda) often exhibited disinviting behaviors, but when confronted in a serious and persistent way, he was willing to change. Sometimes such confrontation can be beneficial to those involved. If intentionally disinviting messages in schools go unchallenged, then schools may move away from their primary function—to invite human potential. Educators who seek to operate from an inviting stance have a responsibility to keep their schools on task.

Level Two: Unintentionally Disinviting

A much larger problem in schools stems from the people, places, policies, programs, and processes that are unintentionally disinviting. Educators who operate at *Level Two* are typically well meaning, but their behavior is often seen by others as chauvinistic, racist, sexist, condescending, or simply thoughtless. Comments such as "What Earl is trying to say" and "It's easy, anyone can do it" typify this level. Professionals who function at *Level Two* spend a lot of time wondering "What did I do wrong?" "Why aren't my students learning more?" "Why is everyone so upset with me?"

Teaching that is unintentionally disinviting is often characterized by boredom, busywork, and insensitivity to feelings. Examples of such insensitivity appear again and again in student accounts of being disinvited: "I feel insulted when faculty sponsors always ask a female to take minutes," wrote one girl. Another student described how she was disinvited by a teacher who said: "You can try out for the part . . . if you really want to." A third student complained that the teacher always used the term "broken home" when he could just as easily have said "single-parent family." Teacher behaviors perceived by students as sexist, racist, patronizing, or thoughtless are likely to be interpreted as disinviting despite the teacher's good intentions.

Level Three: Unintentionally Inviting

Educators functioning at *Level Three* seem to have stumbled into particular ways of functioning that are usually effective, but they have a difficult time explaining why this is so. As good as they are, they usually lack a consistent stance from which to operate. Many so-called natural-born teachers, those who may never have thought much about what they are doing, but who are effective in the classroom, are successful because they are functioning at *Level Three*. They typically behave in ways that result in student feelings of being invited, although the teachers are largely unaware of the dynamics involved.

Professionals who function at *Level Three* are like the early "barnstorming" airplane pilots. These pioneer pilots didn't know a lot about aerodynamics, weather patterns, or navigation. They flew by the "seats of their pants." As long as they stayed close to the ground and the weather was clear so they could follow the highways and railroad tracks, they did fine. When the weather turned ugly or night fell, however, they became disoriented and got lost. In difficult situations, they lacked a dependable guidance system.

The problem with functioning at the unintentionally inviting level is that the educator can become disoriented and unable to identify the reasons for his or her successes or failures. If whatever "it" is should stop working, the teacher does not know how to start it up again or what changes to make in his or her behavior. In other words, the teacher lacks a consistent stance—a dependable position from which to operate. A colleague, Charles Branch, once remarked that he would rather work with people who are functioning at *Level One* than those who are at *Level Three*. At least with Level One you know where you stand. The need for consistency and dependability in professional relationship sets the stage for *Level Four*.

Level Four: Intentionally Inviting

Educators should strive to be intentionally inviting. Doing so requires understanding the reasons for and the results of one's behavior and having the desire to function in a dependably inviting manner. But even at this top level, some are more successful than others in their actions. Here are some possible reasons for degrees of success within the broad category of *Level Four*.

Educators who seek to be intentionally inviting, but who are uncertain about the process, are going through a transition period. (This transitional process is analyzed in the final chapter of this book.) They begin to understand the processes involved and make a conscious effort to be inviting. When they face difficult situations, however, they may resort to lower and perhaps more familiar levels of functioning. Students generally feel good about these beginning *Level Four* teachers, but may have a vague feeling that these teachers are not too dependable and can't be counted on in tough situations. With experience and practice, teachers are likely to move successfully through this transition period. Educators who are dependable in their actions consistently face diverse and difficult situations with a particular stance. The importance of consistency and dependability is illustrated in the following:

Stubborn Teacher

My teacher is so stubborn! She is told that I am unmotivated.

But she invites me anyway.

She is told that I don't want to learn.

She invites me anyway.

She is told that I don't have the ability.

She invites me anyway.

She is told I just want to cause trouble.

She invites me anyway.

She invites me again, and again, and again.

She fills my world with invitations.

One day, I'll take the greatest risk of my life.

I'll accept one, and see what happens.

When educators who are functioning at Level Four perceive, choose, and act with consistency and sensitivity, they are likely to become artfully inviting, a term first used by Tim Gerber, a colleague. At this point educators have integrated Level Four behaviors into what appears to be an effortless activity, but what is actually the product of serious and sustained effort. The process is similar to that gone through by someone who has worked to become fluent enough in a language to think and create in it. Artfully inviting educators think in a special language of "doing with" rather than "doing to." They have developed the ability to approach even the most difficult situation in a professionally inviting manner. When educators who are functioning at this advanced level face problems, they can rely on their understanding of invitational education to develop solutions.

Educators functioning at *Level Four* are like modern jet pilots. Thanks to their knowledge, they can "fly on instruments" around or over dangerous weather fronts. In the final analysis, this ability to chart and maintain a dependable flight pattern makes the difference between success or failure as a professional helper.

Recognition of the ability to be intentionally inviting and the artful use of this ability can be tremendous assets. By understanding the four levels of functioning, by seeking to function at the highest level, and by improving abilities within this level, educators can be powerful forces in inviting school success.

Summary

Invitational education requires the artful blending of teacher perceptions, stance, and behaviors. This involves viewing students and oneself as able, valuable, and responsible and having a positive view of the educative process. Teacher stance represents the teacher's disposition regarding trust, respect, optimism, and intentionality.

Chapter Three concluded with a simple classification procedure for evaluating personal and professional conduct: (a) intentionally disinviting, (b) unintentionally disinviting, (c) unintentionally inviting, (d) intentionally inviting. The next chapter presents the "craft" of invitational education, which includes being ready, doing with, following through, and the choices involved in the inviting approach.

4

The Craft of Inviting

The best teacher is one who, through establishing a personal relation, frees the student to learn. Learning can only take place in the student, and the teacher can only create the conditions for learning. The atmosphere created by a good interpersonal relationship is the major condition for learning.

C.H. Patterson, *Humanistic Education* (1973, p. 98)

Certainly all educators are inviting from time to time, either intentionally or unintentionally. However, those who are perceived by others as dependably inviting possess two important characteristics. First, they hold the point, that is, they consistently function in an inviting manner, even in the most difficult and challenging situations. They reflect unconditional respect for the value, ability, and self-directing powers of those with whom they work. Second, they creatively integrate a variety of skills into the craft of inviting. This chapter looks at a sequence of skills and their artful orchestration to better assist educators in developing this craft.

Invitational education involves blending perception and stance into those activities that are most appropriate for the varied situations in which professionals find themselves. Although no two situations are ever the same, there are skills that teachers and other professionals can use before, during, and after interactions with students and others.

Some cautionary words are necessary when considering craft as the integration of skills. Being intentionally inviting results from basic perceptions regarding oneself, others, and the world and from developing and maintaining an inviting stance. When offering something beneficial for consideration, it is necessary to see the process as fluid. Things may change during the process—even the nature of the invitation. It is vital to pay attention to the purposes of everyone involved.

The skills described in this chapter cannot be formulistically applied to every situation because they are not techniques to move people in desired directions like functionaries in a system. Rather, these skills are principled strategies for developing doing-with relationships. Skills are aids for ethical persuasion and not tools for manipulation. Without this understanding there is always the danger, as researchers (Mahon & Altman, 1977; Patterson & Purkey, 1993; Plum, 1981) have pointed out, that skills can replace dialogue in the interpersonal process. This would be the antithesis of invitational education.

Although techniques can easily be overemphasized, several skills can be valuable to educators. These skills can be learned and improved upon. In an inviting school, teachers have more rather than fewer skills and as a result have more degrees of freedom in working with people. Skills are both useful in themselves as well as a means of systematically developing deeper understandings and more integrated behaviors. The following are three clusters of skills: those associated with being ready, doing with, and following through.

Being Ready

The scout motto "Be Prepared" is a good beginning for developing inviting skills. Being ready helps prevent being overwhelmed and sets the tone for what follows. Two aspects of being ready are preparing the environment and preparing oneself.

Preparing the Environment

The school environment, as Barron (1992), Beane (1991), Lezotte (1989, 1990) and others have documented, is where the student develops his or her positive or negative attitudes about learning and about oneself as a learner. Students receive constant signals from the physical setting of schools, signals that tell them how much the people who design, build, operate, maintain, and manage schools care about them and their learning. For example, one student, describing her school, put it this way: "Yuk! How would you like to spend your whole day in a place that looks like this?" Sadly, teachers sometimes say the same thing.

Preparing an inviting environment involves creating a clean, comfortable, and safe setting in which people who work in schools feel welcome and at ease. Everything in the school counts. Developing an optimal physical environment means working to ensure that rooms, hallways, and commons areas are adequately lighted and heated; have plenty of fresh air, comfortable furniture, living plants, attractive bulletin boards; and are freshly painted. (An often overlooked, but particularly disinviting aspect of schools can be noisy, fluorescent lights that keep buzzing in your head, even after you leave the room.) Adequate supplies are also important, as one teacher explained in this vignette: "One of my five-year-olds is left-handed. Last week I overheard a discussion he had with another student over the importance of having left-handed scissors and cutting well. He then proceeded to ask, 'Mrs. Mancino, didn't you buy those left-handed scissors just for me?'" Even left-handed scissors can be a special invitation.

Educators who understand and practice invitational education find ways to improve the physical environment, even when "nothing can be done about the problem." From an inviting point of view, something can always be done. Challenging defeatist and often self-fulfilling statements is a good beginning.

Berger and Luckman (1966) noted in their classic text, *The Social Construction of Reality,* that people both create and are created by their environments. By that they mean people develop standardized practices for meeting their needs, but get locked into the mindset of these practices: the tools control the workers. Things are done without thought because that is how they have always been done. Those who practice invitational education find innovative ways to break out of lock-step methods in creating and operating schools.

An excellent example of a physically inviting school is Lancashire Elementary School in Wilmington, Delaware. Just a few things principal Fred Michaels and his staff have done include constructing a large sign welcoming everyone to the school, planting a tree *inside* the school, making one hallway into a cave museum, having students bring bricks and build their own road in a side corridor, and decorating the teachers' lounge so that it looks better than most restaurants. Even with these accomplishments, Fred Michaels has said, "We've only just begun!" Another example of a physically inviting school is Celoron Elementary School in Celoron, New York. Charlie Brown, the principal, organized parents, and together they dug a beautiful swimming pool in the basement of the sixty-year-old school. Lancashire and Celoron schools are creative illustrations of people preparing the environment to develop the most inviting place in town.

Preparing Oneself

Becoming an inviting teacher involves recollecting and reflecting on what it was like to be an invited, or disinvited, student. Teachers can deepen their experiential base by recalling specific instances in which they were invited, others in which they were disinvited, then answering these questions: "What happened?" "How did I feel?" "How do I feel now in reflecting on this incident?" "What would I change?" "What inviting and disinviting experiences might students in my classroom be sharing twenty years from now?" Making invitational education personal and concrete removes it from the realm of abstract theory and moral exhortation and assists educators in remembering what it was like when they were on the student's side of the desk.

Educators can prepare themselves to be inviting to all students, especially those from different backgrounds, by examining their own suppositions. One of the most important things that teachers can do in the classroom is become aware of their own biases and stereotypes toward certain students, thus recognizing the influence of these perceptions on the academic performance of students.

Inviting skills are more likely to be successful when teachers are honest with themselves about their own feelings and work to remove negative ones. Martin Haberman (1994) has developed a five-step process that educators can use in addressing their own prejudices.

First, he asks educators to survey their belief systems and list those individuals and groups that they believe to be inferior (for example, other races, those of alternate sexual orientation, the poor, or handicapped).

For those educators who go into denial ("I have no prejudices... what sort of person do you think I am?"), the likelihood is that they will not move from this stance. In such cases, their roles as educators are jeopardized. They are unable to face themselves and become questionable company for young people.

Second, Haberman asks educators to inquire about the sources of their prejudices: "Where did I learn these things, from whom, when, and under what circumstances?"

Third, educators should ask themselves: "In what ways do I personally benefit from my prejudices?" For example, if I am wealthy, do I benefit from tax shelters at the expense of others? If I am of the dominant religious faith, do I benefit from restricting the rights of other religions? This third step is particularly revealing, for it demonstrates how society may encourage certain prejudices.

Fourth, educators need to examine how prejudices influence what individuals hold to be true about children, teaching, learning, and the educative process. Questions to be considered here include attitudes toward tracking, grouping, retention, promotion, penalties, punishments, and the nature of the curriculum. What biases exist regarding gender, race, age, socioeconomic and ethnic background?

The fifth, final, step according to Haberman, is to encourage educators to work out a definite plan to check prejudices, challenge them, unlearn them, and move beyond them.

Teachers who wish to be inviting work at assessing their biases and seek ways in which they can develop greater respect for individual differences and cultural diversity. Some ways of accomplishing this include attending workshops and ethnic festivals and participating in various human relations programs. The result may be greater sensitivity and selectivity in choosing curriculum material. The result may also be more appropriate and caring phrases, examples, jokes, and stories used in the classroom, teachers' lounge, conference center, or wherever professionals gather. With such opportunities available for educating oneself, there is no justification for professionals to be intentionally disinviting.

Going beyond a sensitive and caring approach to individuals, Reed (1992) points out how teachers who seek to be inviting in our multi-cultural society can systematically deal with curricular and cultural transformation. Arguing that a subtle but persistent monocultural undertone is disinviting in process and consequences to an ever-grow-ing portion of the school population, she urges teachers to become advocates for multicultural reform. In the fight against prejudices, teachers cannot be neutral spectators. They should be combatants against the subtle and not so subtle forces that negate the worth and ability of large numbers of their students.

Teachers who seek to be strictly objective in dealing with students are operating from an educationally distorted position. To be objective is to make an object of that which is being studied. Students are more than objects and teachers more than cataloguers. As human beings who seek to make a life in a world that may seek to negate their background, cul-ture, and basic worth, students can be supported by teachers who are on their side and who sense what they experience. Being ready means to proactively deal with realizing the ability, value, and responsibilities of every student.

Doing With

Being inviting is a special way of being with people. After preparing the environment and themselves, educators who desire to be personally and professionally inviting work to develop the following seven skills: (1) developing trust, (2) reaching each student, (3) reading situations, (4) making invitations attractive, (5) ensuring delivery, (6) negotiating, and (7) handling rejection. Each of these will be considered in turn.

Developing Trust

The importance of developing trust in schools has been documented for decades. Recently, Nel Noddings (1984, 1992, 1993) has stressed the importance of students perceiving that they are understood, received, respected, and recognized by teachers. In particular, she emphasizes that teachers demonstrate full receptivity to the other (engrossment) and the furthering of the other's purposes (motivational displacement). It is hard to trust people who seem distracted and only concerned about themselves.

In addition, teachers develop trust by being nonjudgmental, respecting a student's confidentiality, and following through on agreements. One betrayal of trust can destroy the best relationship. This was expressed to us by a graduate student: "When I was in high school, I went to my football coach and shared my feelings about a personal matter. He seemed to listen and respect what I had to say, but at the next practice he kept bringing it up in front of the other guys. I'll never forgive him for that." Once a confidence is violated, it is difficult to reestablish a trusting relationship.

Trust is communicated by a person's entire body. Many researchers have provided ample evidence that we constantly communicate deeper feelings with the language of behavior. Every verbal message (for example, "Welcome to the fifth grade") also has the behavioral message. The nonverbal message may lie in the teacher's tone of voice, physical appearance, body stance, facial expression, gestures, and physical proximity. Eye contact—looking directly at a particular student—especially can signal, "I am sincere in what I say, and my welcome is especially for you." A warm tone of voice, a neat physical appearance, a friendly smile, and direct eye contact all communicate that the student really is welcome. On the other hand, a teacher's aloof behavior, forced smile, tightly crossed arms, or indifferent manner may say more clearly than words, "I would rather not be here with you."

Nonverbal language is so important that a hallmark of inviting teachers is that they ensure that their eye contact, body posture, facial expression, and tone of voice agree with their verbal messages. They appear serious when stating displeasure, they look at a student when expressing sincerity, and they tense their bodies when expressing frustration. Their body language agrees with their spoken language, even in complex situations.

Because students are quick to spot conflicts between what teachers say and how they behave, it is vital for inviting teachers, in Kraft's (1975) words, to "come on straight." Coming on straight means sharing feelings of happiness, anger, enthusiasm, sadness, excitement, or boredom. Teachers who can express their feelings are more likely to be seen as "real" by students. One high school student expressed the importance of real behavior by a teacher with these words: "I remember that our high school history teacher was not afraid to express his feelings. He let us know when our misbehavior was getting to him. But he didn't show just his angry side. Once he cried at the end of a movie shown in class when the hero died. I learned a lot from him besides history . . . that it's OK for a man to express an emotion besides anger."

Coming on straight does not mean unbridled self-disclosure. Obvious advantages are involved in self-disclosure and sharing one's feelings with others, but such sharing should not be overdone. Disclosure, as Johnson (1993) emphasizes, should be relevant to the nature of the relationship and appropriate to the situation. When others casually ask about one's situation, they do not expect a complete medical history. Accepting and applying an inviting approach does not consist of displaying one's every immediate emotion. Just because you may *feel* like being intentionally disinviting does not mean you should be. In other words, coming on straight means taking the total situation into account when displaying feelings, and choosing behaviors that are caring and appropriate to the circumstances.

Self-disclosure is also determined by how comfortable each individual feels in revealing himself or herself to others. People vary in how much they choose to share. Some teachers are more open than others. It is important, therefore, that teachers take their own feelings into account when determining how much of themselves they choose to share with other people and how skilled they will be in the process. At times this may mean letting others know when and why they are uncomfortable about something.

Perhaps the best way to summarize the importance of being real with students is to quote a teacher: "During the real 'up tight' period of the school year following Christmas vacation, I found a note under my classroom door. It read: 'Mr. Maggor, be yourself, don't try to be someone you're not.' It was signed 'A student and a friend.' Suddenly I realized that I had been coming down hard and mean on little things, which was not me and not my usual behavior. Later the two students, neither of whom I had in class, stopped by and talked with me about it. That day I learned a lot about the importance of being myself with my students."

Reaching Each Student

Simply sending inviting messages is not enough. Invitations are a means for personally involving each student in his or her education. Teachers who practice invitational education ensure that their invitations to learning are distributed fairly and sensitively and are received and acknowledged by each student. Teachers tend to communicate a disproportionate number of invitations to some students while neglecting others. The problem of favoritism, exclusion, and their negative influences on both self-concept and school achievement has been documented by McAdoo and McAdoo (1985), Youngs (1993) and many others.

One way to reduce or eliminate favoritism is to send learning invitations systematically. Rather than relying on a random pattern of interaction in which the teacher will most likely call on those students perceived as having the correct answer, the inviting teacher works to ensure that each student is summoned cordially to participate in class. This is accomplished through rotating assignments, seating charts, class rosters, check sheets, card files, or other means. The teacher's attention is equally spread and time is taken for some personal contact with each student each day.

The importance of the time reserved for one-on-one contacts with individual students cannot be overestimated. Although not easy with large classes, it is vital that the teacher squeeze in a few moments for semiprivate chats. These chats may last less than a minute, but they can be powerful incentives to learning. Inviting teachers use odd bits and pieces of time for these brief talks (while waiting for the bell, walking to the car, serving on lunchroom or playground duty, straightening up after class, or storing equipment). This habit of trying to reach all students is particularly important in making contact with the quiet, submissive, subdued student who can easily be overlooked or ignored.

One high school teacher who had several large classes said he developed a weekly plan for reaching each of his students. He took the number of students in each class, divided by five, selected that number of students and made sure he made some personal contact with each of them that day. By the end of the week he had made some personal communication with each student in his classes. He said this system pointed out to him that there were students he would have otherwise missed, and it also gave him a more balanced perspective on what was happening in his classroom and in the lives of his students.

Another way to interact systematically with students is through written correspondence. Whether the teacher calls the process journals, letters, notes, or insight cards, encouraging students to write regular messages of some sort to the teacher is helpful. These messages might consist of questions, reactions, arguments, comments, complaints, or suggestions. Their purpose is to open up a system of written communication between the teacher and each student. Of course, respect for confidentiality and professional ethics should be followed when asking students to self-disclose. The teacher can also send brief, written messages to the students by responding to their notes. Teachers who use this system report that some students who rarely speak in class become eloquent when encouraged to present their thoughts in written notes.

The value of systematic patterns of classroom interaction has been well-documented by several researchers (Brophy, 1983, 1987; Good & Brophy, 1994). They reported that when teachers call on students to read in a patterned instead of random way, so that students know in advance the reading order, stress among anxiety-prone students is reduced and excessive competition (a considerable problem among high socioeconomic status children) is lessened.

One further way to reach each student and to call forth student achievement is to demonstrate a purposeful intentional attitude. Students are more likely to accept invitations to learning when they perceive the teacher as being organized, competent, and prepared for class (Amos, 1985).

Reading Situations

To emphasize the importance of reading situations, Aesop tells in one of his fables how the fox is able to cross the thin ice of a pond while other animals, even those who weigh less than the fox, fall through the ice and drown. The fox's secret is that it *listens* to the sound of the ice. Teachers sometimes fail to listen to the sounds of students. They react without taking the time to hear what students are saying. Such teacher behavior was described by a junior high school student who wrote: "My science teacher tries to be a good teacher, but he never listens to anyone. One day I sat next to him in assembly and he asked me how I was doing. I told him that I had a terrible headache. He replied, 'Fine, fine, fine.' He didn't hear a word I said."

Reading situations is the process whereby the teacher attends carefully to students to understand how his or her invitations to learning are being received, interpreted, and acted upon. This general process has been called by various names, including "active listening" (Gordon, 1974), "resonating with the client" (Rogers, 1967), and "attending" (Egan, 1990). Perhaps the blinded Gloucester in Shakespeare's *King Lear* described the process best when he said, "I see it feelingly" (Act IV, Scene vi). But whatever term is used, this is the process teachers use to understand what is occurring within the student's perceptual world. This calls for *reading behavior backwards*, for looking beyond the student's overt behavior to what that behavior indicates about the student's internal world. For example, a student's bitter complaint of helplessness over an assigned problem may mean that the student is feeling frustration and is asking for reassurance. This skill of reading behavior backwards is so important that Patterson and Purkey (1993) postulated that training teachers to understand how things seem from another person's viewpoint should be a major goal of teacher education programs.

In the final analysis, each individual is the world's greatest authority on himself or herself. Only the person with the pain knows where it hurts. For teachers, this means that their invitations are invariably perceived by students in the light of the students' past experiences. To be asked to wash the chalkboard may be viewed as inviting by one child, but definitely disinviting by another. No two individuals ever share exactly the same past, and no two students ever perceive a teacher's invitation in the same way. To predict the likelihood of an invitation being accepted by a student, one first develops sensitivity to how that message might appear and sound in the eyes and ears of the beholder.

Here is an example of how things appear differently when seen from an internal point of view: "Some years ago I had a high school student who appeared to be very poised and self-confident and who played the guitar with marvelous skill," wrote a teacher. "Yet we could never get him to accept our invitation to perform in public. Other teachers said it was because he felt superior to others in the school. But one day he confided in me that he would dearly love to perform, but stage fright made him physically sick with fear." The skill of listening with care helps teachers understand the personal world of students.

Reading situations also enables teachers to see beyond the games students play. Students fear failure much more than most teachers realize. In trying to avoid failure and the resulting embarrassment, students develop entire repertoires of behavior to convince teachers that they are learning when, in fact, they are not. John Holt (1982) documents the subtleties of this process. Such repertoires include body stance (leaning forward), eye contact (steady gaze), nonverbal behavior (head nodding), and other activities (note-taking, question-asking, and so on). Students also learn that a successful way to respond when they do not think they can answer a question is to delay, hem and haw, or mumble. Even thinly veiled flattery sometimes misleads teachers into thinking that learning is taking place and that students feel good about themselves as learners. That these practices are commonplace is evidenced by research indicating that teacher ratings of students' self-concept-as-learner are significantly higher and more positive than the ratings students give themselves on the same scale (Harper & Purkey, 1993).

In simple language, students learn early to pull the wool over teachers' eyes. Many teachers are aware of such ploys. Indeed, they may have used some of them when they were students! Teachers who adopt an inviting approach use a variety of informal, nonthreatening evaluation techniques and discussions to determine what types of invitations to learning may be necessary and which ones are most likely to be accepted.

Attending to feedback and making the necessary adjustments is an important part of reading situations. This means that the teacher is alert to the faintest signal from students that might indicate their desire to respond to an invitation: clearing of a throat, leaning forward, hand half-raised, eye contact, or lingering after class. Successful teachers are aware of such positive nonverbal signals and take special responsibility for encouraging acceptance. They also take responsibility for doing everything possible to ensure that students who accept their invitations to learning have a good chance of success, for they understand that failure, after taking the risk of accepting an invitation, can have long-lasting negative effects.

Our colleague, Mike Fagan, described teacher efforts to maximize chances of student success this way: "An inviting teacher is like a good quarterback in football. When the quarterback throws a pass to a moving receiver, he tries to 'read the situation' and hit the receiver in full stride to maximize his motion, to get into the energy flow of the receiver and to move with him instead of trying to redirect him." By listening for clues in the variations of student behavior, inviting teachers can get into the flow of student energy, so chances of misunderstanding are minimized and chances of success are enhanced.

Making Invitations Attractive

Not all invitations are created equal. Dependably inviting teachers are aware of this and use this awareness to design and send messages that have a good chance of being accepted. These messages include body language (smiles, winks, and nods) and oral communication (statements that convey appreciation and express affirmation). Factors such as vocal manner, physical space, teacher appearance, and body language all have a significant impact on the communicative process.

Making invitations attractive does not mean that they have to be sugar-coated. Judy Stillion, our colleague, provided this example: "Imagine going to a party where the host offered you a piece of candy, then a jelly doughnut, next a piece of fudge, then a sugar cookie, and finally a cup of sweetened tea to wash it down! This would be hard to stomach." Inviting processes should be as well-balanced as nutritious meals; they should provide a variety of tastes and flavors—sweet, bitter, salty, and sour. Too much of one thing, even a good thing, can be disinviting. This applies especially to compliments and praise.

Praise, for example, should be based on honest performance. Praise generally produces increases in effort, but compliments tossed out to students with little or no justification quickly lose all meaning. One student referred to his teacher as a "dead cat teacher": "If you brought her a dead cat, she would praise it." Many young people simply tune out the frequent verbal praise of adults (Glenn, 1992; Schmoker, 1990), a result probably due to the unrealistic amount of praise distributed by some educators.

The importance of realistic praise was demonstrated more than two decades ago by Rowe (1974c), who found that students ranked poorest by teachers actually received more verbal praise than those ranked best. The reason for which the bottom students were being praised was difficult to determine, however; as much as 50 percent of the praise did not appear to be attached to correct responding. Rowe (1974b) commented that bottom students "generally receive an ambiguous signal system" (p. 298). In other words, what these students did or did not do seemed unrelated to the praise they received. By comparison, top students received less verbal praise, but the praise they did receive was more pertinent to their responses. What Rowe's research means for teachers is that actions taken to encourage academic achievement and self-regard must be realistic and relevant to honest performance. As an example of realistic praise, the teacher might say, "Bill, you've covered a lot of territory today. You've learned the process of carrying numbers. You should be pleased with your progress." In this way the teacher points to an honest success—one hard to dispute even by the most dispirited student.

Invitations most likely to be accepted and acted upon successfully tend to be appropriate for the situation, are specific enough to be understood, and are not overly demanding. A colleague, Bruce Voelkel, pointed out that a *limited time* invitation may be especially useful to educators. An example of a limited time invitation would be a teacher saying to a colleague, "I have only ten minutes before I must attend a meeting, but meanwhile, let's go have a cup of coffee." Such an invitation lets the other person know that he or she does not have to invest a great deal of time and thus makes the invitation easier to accept.

Ensuring Delivery

Invitations are like letters—some get lost in the mail. Unless they are received, they do not count. People cannot accept invitations they have never received. Teachers who are dependably inviting check to see that their invitations are received and acknowledged. Their messages are like registered mail—special steps are taken to ensure delivery.

A good way to ensure delivery is through clarity. Clear, direct invitations are far more likely to be recognized and acted upon than vague or indirect ones. An invitation asking, "Please come for dinner on Saturday evening, October 22, at 8:00 P.M." has a better chance of acceptance than one saying, "Let's get together sometime." In addition, a specific invitation makes it easier for students to recognize and acknowledge invitations: "Mark, what did I ask you to do?" If the teacher's invitation is acknowledged, but still not accepted, at least the cards are on the table. The teacher is now in a better position to understand the situation. Did nonacceptance mean rejection, or does the student need time to consider? If the invitation was rejected, why? How can it be made acceptable? If it cannot be made acceptable, then what alternate invitations might lead to the same results? By ensuring delivery, the teacher can make many choices apparent.

Checking the receipt of invitations is also important because students sometimes do not know how to respond or cannot respond appropriately to a teacher's invitations. Often students would like to accept an invitation to learning, but feel unable to do so. Because of self-doubt ("How could I ever learn this stuff?"), threat ("I'm afraid I'll look stupid if I try"), hostility ("They just want to make fun of me"), fear of disappointing others ("I'm not sure I can live up to her expectations"), or resignation ("I *know* I can't do math"), many students have difficulty in responding to even the most attractive invitations. Knowing this, dependably inviting teachers are patient in their work and do not give up easily. They make sure that their invitations are received and acknowledged. Ensuring delivery is particularly important when working with at-risk students.

Students will sometimes perceive the teacher's invitations in unusual ways. What is sent is not always what is received. The same encouragement may have sharply different meanings to different children, even children of the same age. The shy, insecure child may experience great anxiety at a teacher's invitation to read a story in front of the class. A child with high self-assurance may find the same invitation very appealing. Children with severe behavioral difficulties, or children filled with feelings of anger and frustration, may find acceptance of the most well-meaning invitations from teachers or peers very difficult. One teacher described such a student this way: "Tracy comes to school each day with hands clenched tightly, face in a frown. Nothing ever seems to go right for him. The least thing a child does to him will definitely end in a fight. His peers are always cheating him when playing games. The teacher has never liked him. The work is too hard. He leaves school each day with hands clenched tightly, face in a frown." Needless to say, Tracy is a challenge.

Children like Tracy are likely to hide their innermost feelings, and a teacher's invitations to feel able, valuable, and responsible may appear to be the last things they want. But inviting teachers are not misled. They understand that students who hold negative feelings about themselves face a great risk when they accept a teacher's invitation because they become vulnerable to further hurt. They also understand that, for students who have been consistently disinvited, a handful of invitations will seldom be enough to make an observable difference in behavior. Inviting teachers recognize the problems involved, yet they continue to believe their consistent efforts are worthwhile. Understanding the importance of persistence, they invite again and again and again, filling the classroom with invitations, then checking that these messages are received, acknowledged, and perhaps acted upon.

An elementary school teacher, who is a daughter of one of the authors, provided an example of the value of persistence. This daughter is an excellent teacher, but she almost met her match with "Mary." Mary was a foster child who had been terribly mistreated by life. Her situation was so intense that if the teacher so much as *looked* at Mary, the child would likely "go ballistic."

Day after day the young teacher, almost in tears, would talk to her father: "Dad, you know that invitational education stuff you preach, well, it's not working with Mary!" Week after week went by with little or no success with Mary, and week after week the author encouraged his young teacher to keep inviting. Week after week, he kept hearing, "Dad, Mary lost it again today."

On the last day of school, Mary waited until the other children departed, then brought a beat-up Valentine's Day candy box, in the shape of a heart, up to the teacher's desk, placed it down without a word, and walked out the door. The teacher opened the box (rather gingerly), and inside was a scrawled note, "To the best teacher in the world. Signed, Mary." In some cases, invitational teaching is an act of faith.

Negotiating

Invitational education is a cooperative, collaborative activity that involves the participation of both the sender and the receiver. The sender determines the rules under which invitations are sent; the receiver determines the rules of acceptance. These rules are negotiable. For example, the teacher might say, "Nancy, I would like you to help me decorate the stage for tomorrow's assembly." Nancy replies, "I can't come right now, but I'll come after my conference with Mr. Miller." The negotiation is successfully concluded when the teacher says, "Fine, I'll be looking for you after your conference." Willingness to negotiate is an important part of invitational education and an essential part of the democratic tradition.

In seeking acceptance of an invitation a teacher can subtly communicate, "Will you accept? If not now, when? If not this one, which one?" Willingness to negotiate is most important because some students will not accept an invitation when first offered just to see if the teacher really means it. Inviting teachers do not give up easily. They are consistent and dependable in their stance.

Negotiating is not the simple repetition of the same invitation in the same way, over and over, like a broken record. As Walter Barbe commented in an in-service workshop address, "If you've told a child a thousand times, and the child still has not learned, then it is not the child who is the slow learner." The rejection of an invitation is one indication that the message may benefit by being amended and resubmitted.

Recognizing that an invitation to learning has been rejected, a teacher might ask the student, "If you won't accept this invitation, what invitation will you accept?" The purpose of negotiation is to seek a "doing-with" rather than a "doing-to" environment.

Many teachers at various levels have discovered the value of a contract grading system. Students contract for a particular grade to be earned on the basis of the work they help choose and promise to perform. Another approach might offer the student choices among alternatives that are made as appealing as possible: "You may choose to study vocabulary in small groups or you may play a word recognition game." This confronts the student with firm expectations within a framework of respect.

Negotiating, as Fisher and Ury (1981) point out, is the process of "getting to yes." This involves operating from a principled position and having available a wide variety of choices that coincide with the mutual interests of all involved. This most certainly is a "doing-with" process. Even in the best of negotiations, however, there is no guarantee that an invitation will be accepted, no matter how attractively designed or artfully presented. That is because inviting is a dialogical and not a mechanical process. This introduces the skill of handling rejection.

Handling Rejection

Today the majority of teachers are well trained and concerned with their students' welfare. They teach in schools that reflect a commitment to learning and respect for feelings. Some teachers, however, find themselves in less fortunate situations, swamped with assignments that appear to have little relevance to education. These nonteaching responsibilities often include locker checks, hall-monitoring, money collecting, record keeping, playground supervision, lunchroom patrol, bus duty, and a host of other assignments. Teachers could more easily accept such duties if these responsibilities were not coupled with overcrowded classes, dilapidated facilities, apparently bored and apathetic colleagues, out-of-touch bureaucracies, and, perhaps most painful, disinterested and even hostile students who seem to reject the most well-intentioned invitations. (Chapters Seven and Eight will discuss ways to address these situations.)

Faced with numerous rejections, the teacher can easily become disillusioned, bitter, dejected, and may begin to think: "Why should I continue to invite students? My invitations are not accepted. Besides, they're not listed in our behavioral objectives, exit skills, or learning outcomes!" When this thinking takes over, another potentially great teacher joins the ranks of teachers living a professional half-life. This loss of hope and idealism is a terrible blow to education as well as a major calamity for the teacher. Such tragedies need not happen. When teachers operate with patience and courage, conserving and focusing limited energies at the most effective times, they will not be easily intimidated and overwhelmed by what seem like impossible situations in which their finest invitations are apparently rejected.

It is essential, first, for teachers to consider whether or not their invitations have, *in fact*, been rejected by students. Nonacceptance is not the same as rejection. Even an outright rejection of an invitation may be just the opposite. For example, one beginning teacher invited a student to help him move some supplies after class. "Are you kidding?" the student responded. "I got more important things to do." The teacher was hurt and resentful because he assumed that his invitation had been rudely rejected. Later, he was startled when the student showed up to help. Students accept or reject invitations in their own ways and on their own terms. It is important to understand that acceptances come in many forms. The person extending an invitation determines *what* is presented and *how*, but the person receiving the invitation determines *how* it will be acted upon, and *when*.

Even when an invitation is definitely, unmistakably, absolutely, and without question rejected, it is useful to separate the rejection from the person. Just because a student rejects an invitation does not mean that the student is rejecting the teacher. Each student is not so much against others as for himself or herself. Students may reject, accept, or place on hold invitations for countless reasons that have absolutely nothing to do with the teacher.

One of the most common reasons for rejecting an invitation is the memory of similar invitations accepted in the past, but found less than satisfying. If past invitations have resulted in failure, embarrassment, or humiliation, it is a great risk to accept present ones. Teachers who understand this process are less likely to blame themselves or consider it a personal insult when their invitations are rejected. These teachers head back to the drawing board to develop more appropriate invitations. They are not dismayed, and they are not resigned.

Beyond the psychological reasons for rejecting invitations, there are also environmental reasons. The physical conditions of the classroom and school, lighting, public address system, class size, temperature, general aesthetics, scheduling, and even class makeup of students with varying backgrounds, gender, race, socioeconomic levels, and ranges of achievement—all these contribute to acceptance or rejection.

For teachers, this means working to avoid taking rejection too personally. Students took a long time to arrive at where they are, and they will require time to change. Nevertheless, it is important to remember that everything makes a difference. Any invitation, no matter how small or in what area, has tremendous potential. What appears to be a trifle can, in the right situation, make a significant difference. Teachers have an excellent chance of making a difference when they behave trustingly, reach each student, read situations, create attractive invitations, ensure delivery, and are willing to negotiate. Even doing all of these things will not guarantee that an invitation will be accepted. The only sure way to avoid rejection is not to send invitations. But who wants to be a disinviting teacher in a disinviting school?

Following Through

After the teacher's invitation is extended, received, and acknowledged, it can then be accepted, rejected, negotiated, or put on hold by the student. But the process does not end there; the interaction concludes on the teacher's side of the net. The final moves are made by the teacher who takes responsibility for following through on accepted invitations, analyzing and renegotiating unaccepted ones, and adding fresh ones.

An invitation provides a way of coming together for some worthwhile purpose. Following through begins with the teacher asking himself or herself: Were they with me? Were we able to come together, even for a brief time, in mutually beneficial ways? If the teacher answers yes, the feeling should be a peak educative experience—one of those moments that make teaching so exciting. These moments are to be savored and then stored away, to be brought out later when you are feeling a bit low about teaching.

On the other hand, if the inviting transaction was less than successful, the teacher can examine what happened: Was the invitation unclear or inappropriate, did the student need more time to consider, did it require too great a commitment of time or energy, did the student lack the skills to be successful, or were there other factors that made the invitation unacceptable? Reflecting on what happened is an important way to increase the probability of future success. Schools that seek to be inviting, as described in Chapter Eight, set up ways that teachers can practice and discuss the strategies they are using.

Invitational Choices

The craft of inviting involves not only knowing *how* to invite, but also choosing *when* to invite. Inviting is an uncertain and risky business. Consider the choices and risks embedded in sending or not sending, accepting or not accepting, invitations.

To Send or Not to Send

> *Over thirty years ago, when I was a young girl, I attended a square dance. While there I spied a handsome young man standing alone. After watching him for awhile, I summoned my courage walked over to him and said: "Excuse me sir, do you dance?" He replied "No, I don't know how." And I said: "I'll teach you!" We've been dancing together ever since . . . during our thirty years of marriage.*
>
> **A graduate student, The University of North Carolina at Greensboro**

An invitation is an idea someone had, a choice someone made, and a risk someone took. Inviting others involves risks: risk of rejection, risk of being misunderstood or misinterpreted, risk of being accepted, but having things not work out as anticipated. Each of these risks can be minimized, but because human beings live in a less than totally certain world, risks will always be present. Would the human spirit want it otherwise? The greatest hazards in life are to risk nothing, send nothing, accept nothing, be nothing.

Although people take risks when they invite, there are greater risks in not inviting. Teachers who do not invite may be safe from rejection, misunderstanding, or involvement, but that is not what teachers should be. Students learn that they are able, valuable, and responsible when someone takes the risk of inviting them to feel that way.

In the inviting process, good intentions are necessary, but not sufficient. To be personally and professionally inviting, it is important to ask yourself: Is this the most appropriate and caring action I can take with this person at this time?

Choosing to behave in an inviting manner does not mean constantly sending affirming messages. Sometimes the most inviting thing one can do is *not* send an invitation. For example, inviting a colleague to have a milkshake when you know he or she is trying to lose weight is at best thoughtless, at worse, cruel. An ill-timed, inappropriate, or thoughtless invitation is often perceived as very disinviting. Offering a banner to "the best-behaved class" would be appealing to primary-school children, but the same offer made in a junior high school might be received with horror!

In considering the risks involved in inviting or not inviting, there are two general guidelines. The first is to *listen* and be sensitive to what might be perceived as appropriate and caring behavior. Second, when the evidence seems about equally divided between sending or not sending— send! If people invite, others may accept; if people don't, others can't. The choice to send can make the difference of a lifetime. Older adults, when looking back over their lives, report that they worry more about the things they did *not* do, rather than the things they did (Bennett, 1982). Humans have a finite amount of time for inviting . . . an eternity for not doing so.

To Accept or Not to Accept

And I'd like to thank everybody I ever met in my entire life.

Maureen Stapleton,
Acceptance Speech for Best Supporting Actress, 1982 Academy Awards

The inviting process is an interactive and interdependent activity that involves alternating between sending and accepting. Just as there are risks in sending and not sending, so too are there risks in accepting and not accepting.

Accepting an invitation is another way of saying "I trust you." This trust involves a special risk of vulnerability. Individuals don't have control over other people's trustworthiness, yet by accepting invitations they are placing themselves in the care of others. Ultimately, however, if individuals always choose control over risk, they run the even greater hazard described by Edgar Lee Masters in *Spoon River Anthology* (1922): "For love was offered me and I shrank from its disillusionment; sorrow knocked at my door, but I was afraid; ambition called to me, but I dreaded the chances. Yet all the while I hungered for meaning in my life" (p. 65). He continues by stating, "And now I know that we must lift the sail and catch the winds of destiny wherever they drive the boat" (p. 65). When chances of success are good, Masters seems to say, take the chance.

A guideline for accepting life's opportunities is a willingness to risk. The risk of living in a world where people avoid involvement seems greater than the risk of being hurt. There are reasons, of course, why certain invitations cannot or should not be accepted. A reasonable rule of thumb seems to be the following: Accept those invitations worth accepting and decline the rest graciously. Even the process of not accepting an invitation can be done in an inviting manner.

Understanding the dynamics of sending/not sending, accepting/not accepting has just begun. But in simple terms, it seems to go something like this:

> *If I don't invite, you can't accept.*
> *If you can't accept, you won't invite.*
> *If you don't invite, I can't accept.*
> *If there are no invitations, there is no development.*

Summary

This chapter has presented the idea that the craft of inviting requires commitment, sensitivity, courage, and imagination. Inviting is a complicated process of decoding messages, reaching for meanings, making connections, and recognizing subtle nuances of human interaction. This is no easy task. The craft of inviting is more a journey than a destination, however. No one reaches his or her full potential, yet development is possible and growth can be enjoyable. The next chapter will take the craft of inviting into some of the most difficult and challenging issues educators face.

5

Inviting in the Rain

My criticism of invitational education is that it does not seem to take into account the realities of the contemporary school situation, where poverty (both material and spiritual), crime and apathy have made serious inroads into the minds of both students and parents. At least from where I teach it's a tougher row to hoe than anything I have experienced. The negative influences of media and the dysfunctional family are challenging the schools as never before.

Letter from a teacher regarding the second edition
of *Inviting School Success*

Chapter Five is entitled "Inviting in the Rain" because we recognize that it is difficult to be inviting when "the sun isn't shining" and things aren't going the way one wants. However, difficult as it is to dependably act with respect, trust, optimism, and intentionality, this is exactly what is required to successfully manage the most challenging situations that occur in schools. These challenges include the need to maintain good classroom discipline, the growing demands for safety in the schools, and the responsibility to work beneficially with all students who enter schools, including the at-risk and the physically challenged.

Invitational Education in a Violent Society

Perhaps never before has there been such concern for the safety of students in school. Many educators have on-the-scene knowledge of serious confrontations, fights, and even killings. They have experienced trauma right along with their students regarding horrific school violence. Teachers have also suffered verbal abuse and physical assault in dealing with students, parents, and community members.

Statistics related to violent acts on school grounds support concerns identified by educators, students, and parents alike. A 1989 survey by the United States Department of Justice (USDJ, 1991) indicated that nearly 23,000 students reported they had taken items (guns, knives, brass knuckles, razors, spiked jewelry, and so on) to school that would be capable of hurting an assailant (p. 12). According to Quarles (1989), on average a minimum of 157,000 crimes are committed every day in school.

In a 1993 poll of 2,058 students in grades 6 through 12, conducted by pollster Louis Harris for the Harvard University School of Public Health, nearly 60 percent of students reported that they could quickly get a handgun if they wanted one. Thirty-nine percent said that they knew someone who was killed or wounded by gunfire.

According to Mezzacappa (1993), an act of violence occurs in or near a school every six seconds. In even an all-American city like Milwaukee, 119 school-age children have been killed over a three-year period (NEA, 1993). Evidence demonstrates that a pronounced fear of violence exists among educators, students, parents, and the community at large.

To combat the problem of school violence and promote school safety, educators and the larger community have relied on traditional law enforcement methods. Such methods include placing metal detectors at school entrances, posting warning signs, hiring security guards to patrol hallways and school grounds, building security fences, mounting surveillance cameras, outlawing book bags, locking all school doors and windows except one or two entrances, and conducting unannounced pat-down searches of students and shake-downs of their lockers.

Law enforcement methods rely heavily on surveillance, penalties, and punishments. These measures detract significantly from human dignity and worth. In the school, such methods include student suspensions, expulsions, alternative school placement for offenders, arrests by law enforcement officials, felony charges, and various penalties and fines placed on parents or guardians.

Although sometimes effective, traditional law enforcement methods applied to schools carry major negative side effects. These include possible violations of students' civil rights; sharply reduced instruction time during the school day; a decline in morale of teachers, students, and parents; and a financial burden on meager educational dollars. Let's consider these negative side-effects.

- *Civil Rights Costs:* A democratic society is the result of efforts, often at great personal expense, to ensure the civil rights of all its citizens. These valued rights were not easily obtained, but can be easily eroded, especially by those whose mindset is to fight fire with fire. In fact, the best way to fight fire is with water (Haberman, 1994). Denying students' basic civil rights in the name of law and order works against the democratic ethos that schools are supposed to promote. As Wood (1992) has shown, democratic methods that involve student and community support can be used to help ensure school safety.

- *Educational Costs:* Time on task is a major variable in student learning. Students typically arrive just minutes before their first class. Furthermore, school buses commonly arrive within moments of one another. The result creates a frenzy of activity. Even without the process of screening with metal detectors, human logjams are common at the major entrances of many schools. The time taken each morning to adequately move individual students and their materials through a school metal detector distracts heavily from the length of time devoted to the teaching/learning process. The same is true of locker checks and pat-down searches. Such activities weaken the school academically.

- *Morale Costs:* When students are treated as potential threats, they are likely to behave accordingly. Metal detectors, security guards, surveillance cameras, locker checks, and body searches create a pervasive atmosphere of distrust and apprehension among faculty, staff, students, and parents. Such negative feelings within the school undoubtedly effect morale and the teaching/learning process.

- *Financial Costs:* Although it is difficult to obtain accurate figures, it seems logical that the cost of purchasing metal detectors, sealing all uncontrolled entrances and exits, hiring security guards, and adding other security measures takes away from resources designed to promote student learning. A single walk-through metal detector costs approximately $4,000, and each detector is typically staffed by two to four security officers (Kongshem, 1992). Such staffing, in addition to metal detector maintenance charges, adds to the cost of operation and takes away teaching dollars.

When compared with such powerful-sounding approaches to the educative process as *assertive* discipline, *tough* love, *mastery* learning, and teacher *empowerment*, invitational education may sound weak and ill-equipped to confront the major problems of education. The reverse is true. Inviting behavior is strong; dictating behavior is weak. Educators who rely on dictation are likely to find themselves in difficult straits when confronted by students who also have formidable power. Time-out corners, in school suspensions, corporal punishment, or expulsion are unlikely to impress students who face the harsh realities of grinding poverty, gang warfare, drive-by killings, or bitter inequalities.

Haberman (1994) presents a compelling case for gentle teaching as an antidote for a violent society. He maintains that educators have no choice other than gentle teaching when working with at-risk students. He wrote, "Beyond kindergarten and the first two grades, teachers can no longer physically control their students with external sanctions or fear. For teachers to pretend that they have means which can force students to learn or even comply is a dangerous myth which can make poverty schools as coercive and violent as the neighborhood outside the school" (p. 4). Relying on coercion and force demonstrates little regard for viable alternatives or respect for students; it lacks educational character, intelligence, or imagination. This chapter will first address moderate and typical discipline processes, then move to more serious concerns.

An Invitational Approach to Discipline

Maintaining good discipline in schools has been, and probably always will be, a major concern of educators. Students tend to resist external control because it restricts personal choice and limits freedom. This love of freedom is a valuable part of the democratic ethic and should be cultivated rather than condemned. At the same time, teachers are responsible for maintaining reasonable control in the classroom and for achieving the goals set forth by society. To maintain order (usually called *discipline*), teachers have tried just about everything.

Earlier methods of discipline were essentially negative, with fear and punishment playing major roles. One of the first schoolhouses built in the United States had a whipping post (Manning, 1959) and in the "good old days" many painful techniques were devised to inflict physical punishment on erring students. Fear played a major role in maintaining discipline, and children received ominous warnings from home, school, and pulpit that, as James Whitcomb Riley said in "Little Orphan Annie," "the gobble-uns'll git you ef you don't watch out!" (1916, p. 1170).

Fortunately, more modern methods of maintaining classroom discipline are generally positive (Albert, 1989). Many researchers and writers (Charles, 1981; Curwin & Mendler, 1988; Dreikurs & Cassel, 1974; Gathercoal, 1991; Purkey & Strahan, 1986, Purkey & Stanley, 1994) and others have provided practical tips about how to deal in a respectful and caring manner with student misconduct. Behavior modification techniques that seek to reinforce desirable behavior and extinguish undesirable behavior are often effective. For behavior modification to work, the classroom is usually arranged so that when students behave in desirable ways, desirable things happen to them. Reinforcement of this sort relies primarily on rewards rather than punishments to modify and shape student behavior.

Most contemporary behavioral approaches treat discipline primarily as a matter of employing certain techniques. Invitational education, by comparison, focuses on the larger issues of teacher perception, stance, and action. The teacher strives to develop a fair-minded perspective and works to maintain good discipline through caring and consistent expectations for oneself and for others.

An inviting approach to discipline centers on the dignity of people. Whether intentionally or unintentionally, educators sometimes run roughshod over the personal feelings of students. "My last name is Turley" a student wrote, "and my science teacher always called me 'Turkey' and laughed. At first I felt hurt, and now I'm just resentful." When educators employ tasteless humor, ridicule, and lack of respect for students, it is not surprising that students and their families reply in kind. In practical terms this means that teachers should consistently practice common courtesy and civility and encourage these practices in others. A colleague, Robert "Buzz" Lee, believes this process is so important that he signs a "no-cut contract" with each of his students at the beginning of each semester. This contract stipulates that "I won't disinvite myself, I won't disinvite you. I will invite myself, I will invite you." Everyone is encouraged to sign the contract.

Students who are consistently treated with dignity and respect are less likely to cause problems in the classroom. Wonderful things can happen when students sense they are respected, seen as responsible, and have their feelings considered. Conversely, students who think that teachers are out to embarrass them, and that the system is geared to convince them that they are worthless, unable, and irresponsible, will find ways to rebel, disrupt, and seek revenge—as humans have always done to voice their discontent and resentment. This is powerfully illustrated by the words of Shakespeare's hunchback, Richard: "And therefore, since I cannot prove a lover, to entertain these fair well-spoken days, I am determined to prove a villain, and hate the idle pressures of these days" (*Richard III*, Act I, Scene i). When students feel disinvited in school, they are likely to respond in kind.

Beyond manifesting respect for students, good discipline is developed and maintained by teachers who believe that teaching should be as interesting and involving as possible, and that students should experience honest academic success. When teachers recognize boredom and lack of success as causal agents in misbehavior, they are more likely to seek ways to make their teaching as engaging, exciting, and successful as possible. Everyday discipline problems tend to diminish when students are interested, involved, and succeeding in school.

Finally, the ability to invite good discipline depends on the teacher's perception about what constitutes misbehavior. These beliefs vary considerably from teacher to teacher, school to school, and decade to decade. In 1848, for example, a North Carolina high school listed as misbehaviors boys and girls playing together, girls wearing long fingernails, and boys neglecting to bow before going home! Today, most educators agree that rules should be reasonable, enforceable, and educationally relevant.

Too often in the past, educators attempted to enforce rules that were authoritarian, clearly disinviting, and—like regulations pertaining to hair styles, clothing and jewelry—had little relevance to education. An example of the irrelevance of some control efforts was encountered by one of the authors. A high-school girl was suspended from school because she had dyed her hair a bright blue. The thought flashed through the author's mind that if the principal suspended everyone with dyed hair, there wouldn't be a teacher left. With fewer, more reasonable rules, fewer rules will be broken.

By now the reader may be thinking, "I believe all these things about discipline, but some students still insist on being disruptive." This belief has been around for a long time and certainly has a ring of truth to it. Some students resist any form of control, and concerns about behavior will continue to exist even in the most inviting school environment.

When misbehavior exceeds reasonable limits, educators should ask themselves: "What is happening here? Is the student upset or ill? Are certain factors in the school, such as temperature, class size, or time of day, eliciting misbehavior? How does this student view himself or herself and others in the school? Does the misbehaving student need professional counseling or psychological help? Has this student been able to enjoy honest success experiences in school?" This is also the time for the teacher to consider the reasons for his or her own actions: "Am I concerned about this because of my own insecurities, biases, or prejudices? Have I triggered the misbehavior by employing ridicule, relying on the grade book to maintain discipline, or by screaming, yelling, or haranguing?" When satisfactory and fair-minded answers to questions like these do not excuse or explain the misbehavior, an appropriate consequence is necessary. But even at this point, what educators believe about penalties makes a difference.

If educators believe that penalties should be humane and used sparingly, they will use temporary denial of student privileges rather than public humiliation (writing names on board), corporal punishment, or psychological warfare. Punishment should not give students the resentful feeling of being wronged. The object of a penalty is to encourage the student to reflect on the offense, recognize why it was inappropriate, and take appropriate steps to correct it.

Managing Conflict: Rule of the Five C's

Educators face vexing conflicts and pressurized situations the same as everyone else in society. Practitioners of invitational education seek to handle these challenges in the most decent, respectful, and caring ways possible.

This section on managing conflict explains how to resolve concerns in a principled, effective manner. These concerns may be as minor as a student chewing gum in class or as major as stealing, lying, or confronting the teacher or physically abusing other students. Will the invitational approach work in all situations? Of course not. However, it will give the educator a position from which to operate and a valuable guide for addressing difficult situations.

Whether minor or major, personal or professional, invitational education provides a practical way to resolve the concern at the lowest possible level, with the least amount of time and energy, with the minimal possible costs, and most important, in the most humane and respectful manner possible. To do this, the "rule of the five C's" is used. The rule is to employ the lowest C first and to move upward through higher C's only as necessary. The five C's are *concern, confer, consult, confront,* and *combat.*

Anyone can escalate a conflict or aggravate a problem. It takes trust, respect, optimism, and intentionality to resolve the conflict at the lowest possible C, beginning with concern.

Concern

In any situation that involves real or potential conflict, the educator who employs invitational education first asks himself or herself questions such as these:

- Is this situation *really* a matter of concern?
- Can it be safely and wisely overlooked without undue personal stress?
- Will this resolve itself without my intervention?

- Does this involve a matter of ethics, morality, or legality?
- Is this the best time for me to be concerned about this?
- Are sufficient resources available for me to address this?
- Can this be reconceptualized as a "situation," or, better yet, as an "opportunity"?
- Am I concerned because of my own prejudices, biases, or need to impress people?
- Have I conducted a perception check with a trusted colleague to validate my own interpretation of a situation?
- Is this just one of the inevitable tensions and opportunities involved in living in a contemporary, pluralistic democracy?

Real or imagined concerns in school can often be handled at this lowest level by asking and answering the above questions. The potential conflict may quickly resolve itself.

There are times, of course, when a concern is sufficiently troublesome that it requires action. Then it is time to confer.

Confer

To confer is to initiate an informal and private conversation with another person. The individual who embraces invitational education begins by signaling the desire for a positive and nonthreatening interaction (using the person's name, friendly eye contact, non-aggressive posture, smile, handshake, and so forth). Then the individual briefly explains, in an intentionally nonconfrontive and respectful way, what the concern is, why it is a concern, and what is proposed to resolve it. For example: "Bill, when you come late to class, I spend extra time looking at your admission slip. Please come on time tomorrow. *Would you do this for me?*" Asking for what is wanted is vital. Although the reader may think that the student should do it for himself or herself, it is the teacher's concern that is being addressed. The purpose of the 5-C's is to help manage the teacher's concern "This tardiness is bugging me!" Obtaining commitment from the student by asking, "Will you do this for me" is very important and connects with what follows.

At the conferring level, consider these questions:

- After expressing my concern, have I carefully listened to encourage honest communication?

- Is there a clear understanding by both parties regarding the nature of the concern?

- Do both parties know *why* the situation is a concern?

- Is there room for compromise or reconceptualization? (Perhaps the student is late for class because the bus is running late. This may require action regarding bus schedules.)

- Have I clearly asked for what I want? ("Will you do this for me?") Again, it is important to obtain commitment.

- Is my concern important enough to move to a higher level?

In most situations, a one-on-one, respectful, and informal conference, always in private, will resolve the concern. However, it is useful to record and document the concern for possible future use. In cases where conferring does not solve the problem, consulting is appropriate.

Consult

Consultation is more formal than conferring. Consultation involves clear and direct talk about a concern that has already been discussed and not yet resolved. For example, "Bill, last week *you told me* that you would get to school on time, but this morning you were late again. I expect you to keep your word." Questions to be considered at the consultation stage include these:

- Again, is it clear to both parties what is expected?

- Are there ways that I can assist the student in abiding by previous decisions? (A morning wake-up call for a few days or the loan of an alarm clock might work miracles.)

- Have the consequences of not resolving the situation at this early stage been considered? (Don't wait too long to express valid concerns.)

- Will confrontation resolve the situation? (Is it worth the effort?)

Should consultation, after repeated attempts, not work, then it is time for confrontation.

Confront

Confrontation is a no-nonsense effort to resolve the concern. At this time it is important *again* to explain in detail why the situation is a concern. Now is the time to be direct and frank and to explain why the situation continues to be a concern. Point out that this situation has been addressed previously and repeatedly, and that progress has been insufficient.

It is appropriate and caring at this level to speak of consequences. For example, "Bill, if you continue to come late to class, I will put you on report." Now is the time to move to logical consequences of behavior. Questions to ask at this serious level include these:

- Have I made a sincere effort to manage this concern at each of the lower levels?

- Do I have documented evidence that I have made efforts to resolve the conflict at lower levels?

- Do I have sufficient authority, power, and will to go through with stated consequences?

When the first four levels have been applied in turn, each party is likely to know that the stated consequences are fair and impartial. Should the conflict persist in spite of the first four C's, then the final C level is appropriate.

Combat

At this ultimate level, the word "combat" is used as a verb rather than a noun. The purpose is to combat the situation, not the person. The word "combat" stresses the seriousness of the concern. It also indicates that because the concern has not been resolved at lower levels, this is the time to move to consequences. This requires direct, immediate, and firm action.

Sometimes educators are forced to bypass lower levels and go directly to combat—for example, when one student is physically abusing another. But even here, invitational education warns against unnecessary force, insults, or abuse. A valuable resource for educators is to become acquainted with crisis situations and how to respond to them. Many schools provide this training for faculty and staff.

For obvious reasons, combat situations are to be avoided whenever and wherever possible. At the combat level, stakes are high, and there are likely to be winners and losers. Who wins and who loses is often unpredictable. Moreover, having combat situations requires a great deal of energy that could be better spent in teaching and learning. Yet, when lower C's have not resolved the concern, it is time to enter the arena. Wherever possible, try not to "take the hill without covering fire": try to ensure that previous steps have been taken. In preparing for the combat level, consider the following:

- Do I have clear documentation that other avenues were sought?
- Even at this late date, is there a way to find avenues of compromise?
- Are there sufficient support and resources to successfully combat the situation?

Regardless of the level at which the concern is resolved, the educator who employs invitational education consistently maintains respect, trust, optimism, and intentionality throughout the entire process.

By handling concerns at the lowest possible level, educators who employ invitational education save energy, reduce hostility, and avoid acrimony. By applying the five C's, it is possible, even in the most difficult situations, to manage conflicts. This is a major strength of invitational education: Invitational education can be used to understand and develop strategies for dealing with concerns, up to and including violence in schools.

Understanding Violence

Haberman (1994) has identified at least five factors that set the stage for violence.

1 *Lack of trust in adults*. A general breakdown in adult reliability, intentionality, competence and truthfulness has caused many young people to withdraw from adults and become suspicious of their motives.

2 *Presence of violence*. According to the Carnegie Quarterly (1992), 25 percent of urban, inner-city youth have claimed to have witnessed a murder. This violence is magnified by mass media that fixate on murder and mayhem.

3 *Lack of hope*. Countless young people simply see no hope for themselves. They view themselves as without options and going nowhere, particularly in school.

4 *The presence of mindless bureaucracy*. The system treats teachers and students as functionaries and continually evaluates according to conformity and performance, rather than creativity and effort.

5 *The influence of a culture of authoritarianism*. The use of power and coercion as the perceived way to handle situations is often supported by politicians, press, and public.

Invitational education directly counteracts each of these triggering factors for school violence.

Although there are other reasons why violence exists in schools, these five suggest how factors work together to encourage frustration and elicit aggression in students. The following suggestions are representative of how invitational education can help to promote safety and reduce violence in schools.

Creating and Maintaining Safe Schools

The following twenty-five suggestions are only examples of the many ways educators who employ invitational education can promote school safety and reduce violence.

1 *Teach conflict management*. Everyone in the school, including faculty, staff, students, and volunteers, should receive comprehensive training in stress reduction, conflict management, and crisis interventions. Parent and adult caregiver education programs that provide training for families can also be introduced at various school functions and in special classes for adult caregivers.

2 *Ensure success for all students*. Find as many ways as possible to ensure that *all* students have a reasonable chance of success in *all* school activities, both academic and non-academic. This includes participation in field trips, homecoming courts, athletic teams, cheerleading squads, and various clubs as well as all academically-oriented activities. Providing school success for only a few breeds school violence.

3 *Celebrate effort.* In invitational education, effort is as valued as achievement. Taking the chance, trying new ways, and making the attempt are valued commodities. Trying and failing is vastly superior to failing to try.

4 *Organize a crisis team.* Most school counselors have the professional experience and training to organize, train, and direct teams of students, parents, faculty, and staff in crisis management. Inevitably, emergency events occur. These crises may be natural (weather, fire, flood, and so forth) or societal (an armed intruder, suicide, a student riot, and so on). It is essential that the school have a well-planned, quick-response crisis team in position to provide the necessary emotional support and guidance for students, their families, and faculty and staff.

5 *Organize peer mediation teams.* Helping students learn how to take responsibility and resolve agreements through peer mediation is beneficial. Students can elect those fellow students they believe should become peer mediators for a specific school year. This team of peer mediators can then be trained to work together with fellow students to resolve differences. Disruptive students can choose either staff interventions or a session with the mediation team.

6 *Sponsor Alumni activities.* Having successful alumni return to their alma mater (elementary, middle, or high school) demonstrates that students can achieve their goals and aspirations. Often, when such alumni are encouraged to participate in school activities, they stimulate increased community support for schools and students.

7 *Appreciate cultural diversity.* What better way to learn about other cultures than celebrating holidays from around the world? Many students have a wealth of knowledge related to other cultures. Often, they are eager to share experiences. Such celebrations can emphasize the value and richness of diversity and amplify what is held in common among cultures. But beyond celebration, build an appreciation of cultural diversity in all aspects of everyday life, not just during a special month.

8 *Organize student mentors*. Students helping students promote an atmosphere of encouragement. Older students can help acculturate younger students to new buildings, new rules, and new behaviors. Older students can also help younger students with specific school projects or homework assignments. Such relationships are helpful in at least three ways. First, younger students receive individual attention and encouragement. Second, it suggests that someone is interested in their progress. Third, older students are likely to learn that their actions as role models have a significant effect upon younger students.

9 *Look for causes*. Sometimes the causes of violence in schools lie with systems rather than people. For example, running in the halls, pushing, shoving, and fighting may be triggered by inadequate or inappropriate time periods for lunch, change of class, or bus departure. Changing policies may reduce or eliminate some causes of violence.

10 *Conduct group guidance activities*. School counselors should conduct group guidance activities that emphasize problem prevention. The group activities can promote personal responsibility and self-understanding among students and others.

11 *Use name tags*. Permanent name tags (preferably metal or plastic) can be obtained for every professional in the school. This helps everyone identify who belongs in the school and who does not. Name tags help distinguish those in authority at school and help students quickly identify who they can turn to in an emergency. Some schools have successfully experimented with *everyone* in the school, including all students, having permanent name tags. Bar codes on the tags can be used to purchase lunch or check out library books.

12 *Encourage professionals to dress up*. As police officers, health care professionals, and commercial airline pilots well know, authority and perceived confidence are related to appearance. It is vital that all professionals, in the school look the part. In the inviting school, faculty and staff may mutually decide that some personal comfort may have to be sacrificed for professional appearance. As one teacher explained, "I dress for school like I'm going somewhere important."

13 *Encourage students to dress down*. Stealing is a major concern in many schools. Theft of a student's expensive cap, jacket, or shoes can quickly escalate into an ugly confrontation, with violent results. Warn adult caregivers that it can be dangerous to send children to school with expensive clothing, jewelry, or possessions. Rules for appropriate dress should be reasonable, clearly stated, known by everyone, and reviewed regularly.

14 *Stamp out rumors immediately*. Rumors have the potential to ignite violent reactions. The best way to combat rumors is to continuously provide immediate and accurate information. Rumors spring up when reliable information is lacking. Bulletin boards, newspapers and newsletters, TV and radio stations, school assemblies, and telephone hot-lines can all be used to provide accurate and up-to-date information that helps stamp out rumors.

15 *Stress formality*. Professionals in the school should address students and parents in a formal and dignified fashion. Use Mr., Mrs., or Ms. when addressing or referring to parents. Formality should also be maintained when students, faculty, staff, and parents refer to all school professionals.

16 *Organize Parent Patrol teams*. These teams of volunteer parents and adult caregivers provide role models, increase the safety of the school, and encourage parent involvement. Attractive shirts or school jackets embossed with "Parent Patrol" add to the patrols' visibility at athletic events, school programs, hallway monitoring, and other functions. These parents need proper training and an orientation regarding their exact role. It is also vital that they be properly recognized and honored for their efforts at school assemblies, appreciation banquets, and other activities.

17 *Reprimand in private*. People respond differently when they think others are observing their behavior. When students are to be corrected or disciplined, do this in private. This demonstrates respect for students and may defuse a dangerous situation. (This was stated in the section describing the 5 C's, but is worth repeating here.)

18 *Be a cheerleader*. Provide consistent encouragement to students who are experiencing difficulty. Emphasize what they are already doing well, things they might do better, and how they might do it.

19 *Slip the punch*. It is important to know how to "slip a punch" and avoid a flat-out confrontation with students, particularly in the presence of other students. Try to defuse or redirect the student's energy by using patience. Avoid contradicting what an angry student says. Accepting feelings is not the same as agreeing with them.

20 *Avoid the escalator*. Some educators make the mistake of trying to enforce desired behavior by escalating threats of punishment. This can cause the educator to make threats that cannot be carried through (for example, "You are never coming back in this classroom!"). Work to remain calm by slowly exhaling breath.

21 *Use the moniker*. Remember to use students' preferred names at every opportunity. A person's unique and personal name, when pronounced precisely and appropriately, can significantly influence relationships.

22 *Move from celebration to civilization*. Honoring multicultural holidays and heroes through special celebrations is a great way to encourage appreciation for diversity, but these activities are not sufficient in and of themselves. It is vital that schools address the symbolic webbing of the school: The school's position regarding integrating multicultural perspectives into every facet of school life, including places, policies, programs, processes, and the actions of those who live and work there.

23 *Be aware of paraverbals*. The three paraverbal components are tone of voice, volume of voice, and the rate of talking. When working with an angry person, try to use a gentle tone of voice, a moderate volume, and a slower rate of talking. The way an educator responds to a person who is beginning to lose control can increase or decrease the likelihood of verbal or physical aggression.

24 *Maintain a nonthreatening physical stance* An open body stance, with relaxed posture and your body slightly at an angle from the other person, will convey a message of compromise and conciliation. Avoid crossing arms, pointing fingers, or moving too close to the angry person. Give the other person personal space by adding distance between parties.

25 *Let them climb "emotion mountain."* Where possible, when someone seeks to express a strong emotion, let the person vent without any interruption (lecturing, contradicting). Allowing the person to climb emotion mountain—to express feelings—sets the stage for dialogue. Blocking the climb only adds frustration.

These twenty-five suggestions are illustrative of the many ways educators who incorporate invitational education can help prevent school violence and encourage school safety.

People turn to violence when socially-acceptable avenues of expression are unavailable. It is imperative that schools send the signal to all students, in as many ways as possible, that they are able, valuable, responsible, and capable of acting accordingly.

Summary

Because the "sun is not always shining" in schools, this chapter looked at how invitational education addresses difficult situations. A noncoercive perspective was provided to counteract violence in schools and a framework was offered for managing conflict. Twenty-five practical strategies showed the subtle, but persistent strength of the inviting approach. Chapter Six will look at ways of developing this strength in those who wish to apply invitational education.

6

The Person in the Process

Attention to the beliefs of teachers and teacher candidates should be a focus for educational research and can inform educational practice in ways that prevailing research agendas have not and cannot.

M. Frank Pajares, Teacher's Beliefs and Educational Research: Cleaning up a Messy Construct, *Review of Educational Research* **(1992, 62, 329)**

This chapter looks at the person in the process and considers what is necessary to sustain the desire and energy to function at an intentionally inviting level—to develop the stamina and courage of the long-distance inviter. Being professionally inviting cannot be maintained if it is seen as an isolated series of behaviors an educator performs when he or she comes to school. Invitational education can easily be corrupted by those who have learned its techniques but not its stance. As our colleague Charlotte Reed pointed out, "Invitational education is only one aspect of invitational living."

Living the inviting process involves orchestrating four basic areas: (1) being personally inviting with oneself, (2) being personally inviting with others, (3) being professionally inviting with oneself, and (4) being professionally inviting with others. The educator who successfully employs invitational education balances the demands of the four areas and integrates them into a seamless pattern of functioning. Concentrating too much effort in only one or two of the four areas creates an imbalance.

From an invitational viewpoint, quality education is the product of developing and using oneself in creative ways. The inviting educator can balance and orchestrate the demands of these areas, thereby facilitating optimal personal and professional development in oneself and others. These four areas suggest ways to increase one's "IQ" (Invitational Quotient).

Being Personally Inviting with Oneself

Many people go throughout life committing partial suicide—destroying their talents, energies, creative qualities. Indeed, to learn how to be good to oneself is often more difficult than to learn how to be good to others.

Joshua Liebman, *Peace of Mind* (1946, p. 46)

Countless educators are dedicated, caring, and hardworking, but also experience chronic discouragement, dejection, and frustration. These feelings are summed up in the single word *burnout*, defined by Edelwich (1980) as the "progressive loss of idealism, energy, and purpose" (p. 14). Sometimes burnout is self-inflicted. Educators who overlook their own welfare are more likely to experience stress-induced illness. Avoiding boredom and isolation, principal components of burnout, are essential in maintaining an inviting stance.

When professionals constantly sacrifice their own wants and needs to meet the demands of others, the sacrifice gradually builds resentment. Teachers have a moral obligation to their students to take care of themselves. This opinion was supported by Knowles (1977), who points out that although more than 99 percent of us are born healthy, many of us later become ill as a result of personal misbehavior and self-abuse. Knowles believes that we have "a public duty" to preserve our own health. Thus, if one aspires to go the distance, to be a long-distance inviter, it is vital to view and treat oneself and one's potential positively.

Being personally inviting with oneself is a tremendously important enterprise for teachers. It is difficult to invite others if educators neglect to invite themselves. If educators believe that the inviting process is important, then they should apply this belief to their own lives—to stand tall, dress well, eat less, become involved, exercise, and find ways to be fully *present* in this world.

In being personally inviting with yourself, keep in mind that the principles of respect, optimism, trust, and intentionality most useful for inviting others also directly apply to inviting yourself. The most important principle is respect for yourself and your feelings. For example, if exercising at night after a hard day of teaching feels terribly difficult, try inviting yourself to exercise in the morning. If this doesn't work, a self-invitation to play a sport, join a health club, buy an exercise bicycle or minitrampoline, or take a long walk each morning or evening might accomplish the same thing. The goal is to send self-invitations that are most likely to be accepted and acted upon. By listening to your own feelings and by varying self-invitations the probability of success is increased.

Although it is beyond the scope of this book to go into detail about the countless ways of being personally inviting with yourself, here are some suggestions for maintaining your own personal energy level and nurturing yourself physically, emotionally, and psychologically:

Take pleasure in stillness. Too much isolation can be bad, but taking time to be alone is helpful. Enjoy silence. Contemplate and meditate on who you are, where you came from, and where you're going. Being at one with yourself can be deeply rewarding.

Keep in reasonable shape. Maintain physical health. Whether you choose an individual effort (long walks, jogging, exercising, gardening) or an organized sport (bowling, tennis, racquetball), it is important to maintain the body in which one lives.

Plan a long life. Take personal responsibility for your own life support system. Be choosy about what and how much you eat. Eliminate cigarettes and other injurious substances. Maintain health care, look both ways when crossing a one-way street, and fasten your safety belt. The greatest proportion of health and safety care one receives is self-administered.

Give yourself a celebration. Make a pledge to do something special for just yourself in the immediate future. It might be a bubble bath, a fishing expedition, a good novel, a shopping trip, a new outfit, a favorite meal, a round of golf, attending a film or play; celebrate!

Recharge your batteries. Handle short-term burnout by talking things over with a friend or counselor whom you consider to have good sense. Just talking about concerns helps avoid accepting a lot of guilt and anxiety. A good friend or professional counselor can help you find ways to invite yourself.

Live with a flourish. Find satisfaction from many sources, such as a hobby or activity unrelated to your professional life. As much as realistically possible, surround yourself with things you like. Laugh a little. Take a few risks, travel, and assert yourself. Avoid drabness.

One additional way teachers might invite themselves personally is by taking time to remember what it was like to be a child and letting their own feelings find expression. The death of a child is tragic, so why kill the child in yourself? Keep the zest for living alive by trusting your feelings, by being open to experience, by being gentle with yourself, and, when necessary, forgiving yourself. After all, errors are primarily sources of information. If one path does not take you where you wish to go, at least you've learned not to take that path again.

Being Personally Inviting with Others

The next important area in becoming a long-distance inviter is being *personally* inviting with others. Most human interactions have a basic process of interdependence: The greatest life support systems are relatives and friends, and invitational education places a high priority on personal relationships. Professional success, no matter how great, cannot make up for lack of success in personal relationships. It is important to cultivate and treasure a circle of trusted friends and acquaintances as well as to seek out new relationships and explore fresh interests.

A most important aspect of inviting others personally is being "real." Johnson (1993), Rogers (1965, 1967, 1980) and Jourard (1964, 1968, 1971, 1974), among others, have emphasized the importance of appropriate self-disclosure in interpersonal relationships. Disclosure begets disclosure, and it often helps to share personal feelings, to acknowledge that everyone wakes up on the wrong side of bed, goes in the wrong bathroom, and forgets appointments.

One additional aspect of inviting others personally is to develop and maintain unconditional regard and respect for other human beings. As discussed earlier, comments or behaviors that are perceived by others as demeaning, insulting, sexist, or racist are usually interpreted as disinviting regardless of one's intentions. Kidding others about their physical appearance, behavior, background, or misfortunes can be very disinviting. Saying "I was only kidding" may not be sufficient to repair the damage of a cruel jest. As someone commented, "Sticks and stones may break my bones, but words will surely kill me." Here are some practical ways to avoid lethal statements and to be personally inviting with others:

Promote civility. Common courtesy is a most important tool in invitational education. This is usually accomplished by greeting others by appropriate name, showing respect by being prompt with appointments and commitments, promoting "please" and "thank you," and in general demonstrating basic concern and appreciation for others and their feelings.

Let people know you care. Often a get-well card is sent to those who are ill, but a welcome back note is overlooked. A thoughtful birthday, holiday, congratulatory, or other card or note to relatives, colleagues, students, and friends lets them know that they are in your thoughts.

Warm up the class. At the beginning of each class period, a personal greeting, a little light humor, a brief comment on world events, or an inquiry into how things are going can set the stage for learning. Just as joggers should limber up their muscles before jogging, teachers should limber up their classes before teaching.

Break bread together. One of the oldest forms of community is sharing a bit of food and drink. By arranging for something during break or other appropriate times, you set the stage for facilitating good feelings and friendships.

Keep things simple. When someone comes with a complaint, avoid second level problems, such as an angry exchange or counter complaints.

Focus on what the person is saying, listen carefully, and be willing to express regret (this is not the same as an apology). If possible, take some positive action to let the person know that at least you listened and understood his or her feelings.

Stay abreast. Make a special effort to enter the world in which today's student lives. Keep abreast of contemporary fads, fashions, heroes, films, sports, actors, singers, and other current student interests. Using an example from real life can be both personally and professionally inviting.

Positive beliefs about people, coupled with personally inviting behaviors, are basic to invitational education. Yet, as important as it is to be *personally* inviting with oneself and others, it takes even more effort and skill to become *professionally* inviting. This leads to the next two areas—being professionally inviting with oneself and being professionally inviting with others.

Being Professionally Inviting with Oneself

It is difficult to overestimate the importance of being active in one's own professional development. The educator who does not invite himself or herself to grow professionally runs the risk of becoming obsolete. Teachers should continue to be actively engaged in upgrading their skills and knowledge and working to sustain their professional enthusiasm.

Teachers can grow professionally in many ways. Especially challenging is to develop a model of teaching as advocated by Goodman (1988) and Pajares (1992). Teachers can get locked into a certain style of teaching, especially if they have experienced some success with it. Being in a rut, even a successful one, narrows perspective and diminishes professional vitality. The following list represents suggestions for discovering new approaches to being professionally inviting with yourself:

Participate in programs. In addition to typical academic courses, programs, and degrees, special conferences and workshops can provide exciting ways to sharpen skills, learn techniques, and develop new understandings. Attending such professional activities will help upgrade skills and knowledge. You can often find funds to attend developmental activities by contacting PTAs, governmental agencies, business partners, and philanthropic foundations.

Spend time reading. Countless professional books, journals, magazine articles, newsletters, monographs, and the like are expressly written to help educators develop professionally. Finding some time each day to read is an excellent way to stay abreast.

Join professional groups. Be active in professional societies. Working within these organizations to ensure that they maintain high professional quality is important in strengthening yourself professionally as well as aiding the profession.

Conduct projects. Some educators might assume that research should be left to scientists in laboratories, surrounded by computers and data sheets. But bigger is not necessarily better. A teacher's quiet investigation of some question can have a long-range influence on life in and around schools.

Write papers. A valuable way to invite yourself professionally is to write for professional publication. Not everything written must appear in national journals. Numerous local, state, and regional newsletters, journals, and related publications welcome contributions from educators in the field.

Arrange a date. Are there people in your professional world who you admire and would like to know better? If so, be brave! Invite them to lunch. If you invite, they may accept. If you don't, they can't.

Seek feedback. At regular interviews and at the end of each semester seek suggestions from students or others who may be familiar with your work. Find out how they evaluate your teaching and what you might do to make it better. This way you can be showing respect for the opinions of others while strengthening yourself professionally.

Personal and professional growth ultimately culminates in being better able to be professionally inviting with others.

Being Professionally Inviting with Others

From the position advocated in this book, the primary purpose of education is to summon people cordially to realize their potential, meet the democratic needs of society, and participate in the progress of civilization. This is best accomplished by building on the three areas already considered. When these three are functioning at an optimal level, the stage is set for being professionally inviting with others.

Practical strategies for inviting others professionally are so numerous that they have been compiled in a separate book: *The Inviting School Treasury* (Purkey & Stanley, 1994). The *Treasury* is a desk reference that provides more than 1,000 concrete suggestions arranged under 110 topics with 600 cross-references. Each suggestion is designed to improve student academic achievement.

Because the process of being professionally inviting with others is the central focus of this book, it is necessary to go into greater detail in this area. The examination of the fourth area uses self-concept as a springboard.

Earlier, reviewed evidence indicated a significant relationship between self-concept and school achievement. Students' perceptions of themselves as learners apparently serve as personal guidance systems to direct their classroom behavior. A professional understanding of self-concept theory coupled with skills for interpreting how students view themselves as learners are important tools for teaching.

Ways to be professionally inviting with others are suggested by research provided by the *Florida Key* (Purkey, Cage & Graves, 1973), an inventory of student behaviors designed to infer students' self-concepts as learners. The *Key* has been used since 1972 to compare disadvantaged and nondisadvantaged pupils (Owen, 1972), analyze professed and inferred self-concepts of students (Graves, 1972; Harper & Purkey, 1993), compare Caucasian and African American students (Finger, 1995), to study students identified as disruptive and nondisruptive (Branch, 1974), and determine the efficacy of invitational education (Stanley & Purkey, 1995).

The *Key* limits itself to the situation-specific self-concept that seems to relate most closely to school success or failure: self-as-learner. In making deductions about self-concept, most researchers have focused on global self-concepts rather than on situation-specific self-images, such as self as athlete, self as family member, self as learner, or self as friend. By observing only global self-concept—which is many-faceted and contains diverse, even conflicting, subselves—investigators have sometimes overlooked the importance of these subsystems.

In the *Key* research, four factors that relate significantly to school performance were derived through factor analysis. These factors were labeled (1) relating, (2) asserting, (3) investing, and (4) coping. Examining these four factors is useful, for they suggest ways in which educators may be professionally inviting with others.

Relating

The first factor identified on the *Key* as having the greatest significance to the self as learner is *relating*. As measured by the Key, the relating score indicates the level of trust and appreciation that the student maintains toward others.

Students who score high in relating identify closely with classmates, teachers, and school. They express positive feelings about learning, and they think in terms of *our* school, *our* teachers, and *my* classmates (as opposed to *the* teacher, *that* school, or *those* kids). Getting along with others is easy for those who score high on relating. These students take a natural, relaxed approach to school life. They stay calm when things go wrong, and they can express feelings of frustration or impatience without exploding.

Students who score low on relating seem unable to involve themselves in school activities or with teachers and other students. One teacher depicted such a student as follows:

> *Two summers ago, I tutored children who were having problems learning to read. Looking back, I can see how their reading problems were related to how they saw themselves. One boy, John, who was ten years old, was not well liked because of his habit of criticizing others to make himself feel important. His poor self-concept and failure to relate to others were graphically illustrated one day when a huge whipped cream fight was held on an empty hilltop. Whipped cream filled the air for twenty minutes or so as forty kids, each with*

two or three cans, went wild. After the cream had settled, and later that day, John told me he had to spray whipped cream on himself as no one else made a point of doing so.

To be ignored, even in a whipped cream battle, can be a most painful experience.

To be overlooked or ignored by others is an intolerable situation for most people, and they will go to great lengths to gain acceptance. When the desire for positive human relationships is unfulfilled in conventional ways, students are likely to try less conventional or socially unacceptable ways. For example, according to Cartwright, Tomson, and Schwartz (1975) and others, the potential delinquent joins a gang to gain a feeling of status denied by the larger society. This phenomenon has been echoed by Hull and Young (1993) who reported that alcohol is used by social drinkers and alcoholics alike to reduce feelings of personal failure, isolation, and worthlessness.

The following passage from *Manchild in the Promised Land* by Claude Brown (1965) illustrates the pathetic efforts of one young girl to buy human relationships:

> *I found out that Sugar would bring candy and pickles to class and give them to Carole, so Carole liked her and wanted me to like her too. After I got used to Sugar being ugly and having buckteeth, I didn't mind her always hanging around, and I stopped beating her up. Sugar started coming around on the weekends, and she always had money and wanted to take me to the show. Sometimes I would go with Sugar, and sometimes I would just take her money and go with somebody else. Most of the time I would take Sugar's money then find Bucky and take him to the show. Sugar used to cry, but I don't think she really minded it too much, because she knew she was ugly and had to have something to give people if she wanted them to like her. I never could get rid of Sugar. She would follow me around all day long and would keep trying to give me things, and when I didn't take them, she would start looking real pitiful and say she didn't want me to have it anyway. The only way I could be nice to Sugar was to take every-thing she had, so I started being real nice to her (p. 55).*

Literary descriptions as well as scientific research clearly show that human relationships profoundly influence self-concept and school achievement. Although forcing students to relate to each other in positive and productive ways is undesirable and probably impossible, teachers can create an enabling atmosphere in which relating is facilitated. Adelman and Taylor (1993) have documented the importance of an enabling component in human learning, as have Haberman (1994) and Noddings (1992).

A specific teacher behavior that invites feelings of belonging in students is the use of "we" statements to suggest group membership. Encouraging students to involve themselves in school activities promotes a feeling of *our* curriculum, *our* decorations, *our* rules, *our* efforts to keep things clean. Instructional programs can be developed and presented in ways that encourage students to play a cooperative part. Cooperative learning (Johnson & Johnson, 1989) has demonstrated the value of working together to enrich academic achievement while improving interpersonal relationships.

Finally, creating the proper atmosphere for relating involves removing barriers. Skill is necessary to avoid a mismatch between the communication system of the classroom and that of the minority-group student. Teachers may be unintentionally disinviting when they appear to be condescending, patronizing, or over-friendly. "That English teacher tries to be helpful," a student commented, "but she always talks about how 'you Blacks can be proud of what you've done.' It shows me that she is constantly aware of the differences and thinks in terms of labels." Teachers who want to be inviting with others work to avoid expressions and actions likely to be offensive to minority-group members. This requires sensitivity to how things seem from the other person's point of view. Teachers who understand the importance of relating work to remove barriers and to encourage positive relationships in the classroom.

Asserting

> *That which gave me most Uneasiness among those Maids of Honor, when my Nurse carried me to visit them, was to see them use me without any Matter of Ceremony, like a Creature who had no Sort of Consequence.*
>
> Jonathan Swift, *Gulliver's Travels* (1726/1961, p. 95)

The second factor identified in the *Key* research, *asserting*, describes another aspect of self-concept-as-learner—the one that characterizes students' sense of control over what happens to them in the classroom. Students who score high on the asserting factor speak up for their own ideas and are not afraid to ask questions in class. They actively participate in school activities and talk to others about their academic interests.

The importance of asserting oneself has been stressed by Alberti and Emmons (1990) who define assertive behavior as those personal actions that enable one to act in one's own best interests, to stand up for oneself without undue anxiety, to express one's honest feelings comfortably, and to exercise one's own rights without denying the rights of others. Alberti and Emmons view assertive behavior as affirming one's own rights (in contrast to aggressive behavior, which is directed against others) and the "perfect right" of every individual in interpersonal relationships. Beyond affirming one's own rights, assertive behavior also involves the ability to express feelings of positive regard, appreciation, and love—to let others know their presence invites a celebration.

Advantages of assertive behavior have been documented by research (Cotler & Guerra, 1976; Seligman, 1975, 1990). Seligman, who has formulated theories of learned optimism and learned helplessness, states that the experience of internal control is essential to both positive self-esteem and good psychological health. Negative self-regard and psychological depression are the likely results of feelings of helplessness. The problem with learned helplessness is that when one learns to believe that one lacks control, this belief persists even when circumstances have altered so that it does become possible to assert oneself. As Seligman (1990) has documented, optimists do better in school and succeed more at life tasks. One's optimistic feelings of control over what happens to oneself as a student are strongly related to school success.

Assertive behavior can be learned, as Alberti and Emmons (1990) have demonstrated, and can be taught by teachers who invite dialogue and expression of different viewpoints in the classroom and who respect the students' right to express these viewpoints. Class activities that stress moral reasoning, democratic decision-making, and cultural appreciation have been strongly advocated by Bennett and Novak (1981), Berman and LaForge (1993), Kohlberg (1969), Kohlberg and Turiel (1971), Lappé and DuBois (1994), Lickona (1991), Novak (1994), Wood (1992) and others. Many teachers have used such activities to encourage students to explore their own values, rights, and responsibilities.

Teachers can also encourage assertive behavior in their students by teaching them how to express themselves in socially acceptable ways without aggressing against others or denying others' rights. Some children learn to assert themselves early, as evidenced by the words of a little girl, overheard on a playground: "Just because I don't know how to jump doesn't mean that I always have to turn the rope!" Significant differences exist between assertion and aggression. Both teachers and students benefit when they understand these differences and employ assertion rather than aggression in interpersonal relationships. When students are encouraged to assert themselves in socially acceptable ways, their feelings about themselves and their abilities are likely to improve along with their academic performance.

A way to encourage student assertion is to teach students how to avoid or bypass roadblocks to learning. A big problem for many students, especially those who are highly anxious, is what to do when they do not know the correct answer. In oral reading, a student who does not know a word will usually stammer, stutter, and suffer painful pauses until the teacher or another student supplies the answer. Much of this effort is counterproductive and can sometimes be avoided if the teacher invites students to jump over the difficult problem and keep going. In oral reading, for example, the student can bypass the unknown word by replacing it with the words *hard word* and keep going. In a multiple choice test, the student can be told to select an option and move on. The important thing for a student is not to get blocked or hung up on an endless regression that often leads to lowered performance and self-confidence.

One final method useful in enabling students to assert themselves is to show them that going from something to something is much easier than going from nothing to something. By getting started, even if the start is poor, students begin their journey toward improvement and quality outcomes. Contrary to the standard advice that "If it's worth doing, it's worth doing well," encouraging students to do things poorly, at least in the beginning, may be helpful. Doing things well results from first doing things poorly.

Investing

The third factor identified by the *Key* research is the creative part of self-concept-as-learner: *investing.* This factor encompasses student willingness to speculate, guess, and try new things. Students who score high in investing seek out things to do in school without the prompting of extrinsic rewards such as tokens, gold stars, grades, points, or praise. Their reward appears to be the activity itself. Teachers can encourage students to invest themselves in learning by posing open-ended questions.

Open-ended questions do more than require students to regurgitate known facts. Open-ended questions are varied and interesting and ask students to interpret meanings, give opinions, compare and contrast ideas, or combine facts to form general principles. Here are a few examples: What would it be like if we were all born with only two fingers on each hand? What if the South had won the Civil War? What if the earth's axis shifted five degrees? What if the supply of oil was exhausted? What if a license were required to have a child? What if the world became a one-party democracy? Or, even more simply, "What is justice?" "Loyalty?" "Happiness?" "Truth?" Such questions can stir student imagination, create excitement in the classroom, and encourage all students to invest themselves in the discussions. Asking provocative, open-ended questions is an excellent way to summon student investment in learning, particularly when the questions are followed by sufficient wait-time. Dependably inviting teachers use a variety of methods to encourage investing. Some of these techniques are presented in Appendix A.

Coping

Coping, the fourth and final factor identified by the *Key* research, indicates how well students seem to be meeting school requirements. Students who score high in this area apparently possess an image of themselves as able and willing to meet school expectations. They believe in their own academic ability and take pride in their classroom performance. They usually pay attention in class, do their work with care, finish what they start, and expect success from their efforts. Students who score high in coping have discovered and use an important tool of learning: reading. They often pursue reading independently, even when it sometimes interferes with other school activities.

Coping is another name for school success, a subject emphasized throughout this book. What has not been sufficiently emphasized is that no single factor is more relevant to feelings of coping than the act of coping itself. By successfully coping with school expectations, students develop a sense of competence. "I know I can spell," an elementary school student wrote. "I got a good note one time." This sense of competence is a significant part of positive self-regard.

The feeling of competence gained through doing something that works is particularly valuable for children in the elementary grades. When children are successful at leading a class activity, giving a weather report, passing out material, collecting milk money, taking the roll, delivering a note, or storing playground equipment, they are using learned skills to do things that work.

Things that work in higher grades include planning and preparing a complete dinner in home economics, plotting a lot in math class, changing spark plugs in auto repair class, reading a French menu in a foreign language class, or executing a double reverse in football. One student described the process of learning something that works as follows:

> *My first two years at school I was terrible at physical education. "Any girl can kick better than you," I was told. I was always picked last for kickball teams because I could not kick the ball into the air (a firm rule was no grounders). On one particular day in third grade, my teacher, who was sitting with another teacher watching the game, saw that I was soon about to take my turn and undoubtedly kick grounders until I was out. This lady (all six feet of her) called me aside and showed me how to kick under the ball. When I got up to kick, the ball sailed in the air! I'll always remember that teacher who took the time to show me that I could do something that works!*

Any honest success experience, no matter how small or in what area, helps students discover that they can cope with life's expectations.

There are times, of course, when students are not coping and it is necessary to point out their errors. But teachers should not view this as an inconsequential act. Pointing out mistakes, as Dewey believed, "should not wither the sources of creative insight. Before individuals can produce significant things, they must first produce" (cited in Hook, 1939, p. 19). As Elkind (1981) indicated, the stress from fear of failure makes it difficult for children to take the risk of learning. In the classroom, this means that to do things well, students must first *do.* Dependably inviting teachers recognize that experience emerges from inexperience, and that learning is a process of trying things out and finding what works and what does not.

Rather than focusing on mistakes and criticizing poor performance, teachers who are dependably inviting encourage students to feel confident in coping with errors and overcoming them. One high-school girl told how this was accomplished for her: "I was being auditioned for a part in our high-school musical. I was very nervous and worried about getting the part. At the end of my song my voice cracked and I thought my acting and singing days were over. The director looked at me and smiled, saying 'Let's just hope you hit that note on opening night.' It was definitely the warmest feeling I've ever experienced." When students understand that making mistakes is normal, expected, and understandable, they can develop positive and realistic self-concepts as learners.

The four factors of the *Florida Key*—relating, asserting, investing, and coping—identify techniques that teachers can use to enable students to develop positive self-concepts as learners as well as to encourage academic achievement.

Summary

Chapter Six has highlighted the importance of the person in the process. Four basic areas of functioning were presented: being personally inviting with oneself, being personally inviting with others, being professionally inviting with oneself, and being professionally inviting with others. The successful educator is one who artfully blends and synchronizes the four areas and can thus sustain the energy and enthusiasm of the long-distance inviter. The chapter concluded by identifying practical strategies for inviting school success built around the four dimensions of the *Florida Key*: relating, asserting, investing, and coping. Chapter Seven will present two models for next century schools.

7

Two Models for 21st Century Schools

Community is the tie that binds students and teachers together in special ways, to something more significant than themselves: shared values and ideals. It lifts both teachers and students to higher levels of self-understanding, commitment, and performance—beyond the reaches of the shortcomings and difficulties they face in their everyday lives. Community can help teachers and students be transformed from a collection of "I's" to a collective "we," thus providing them with a unique and enduring sense of identity, belonging, and place.

Thomas J. Sergiovanni, *Building Community in Schools* (1994, p. xiii)

Just as students possess relatively untapped potential for development, educators possess relatively untapped potential for encouraging this development. This book has emphasized what the individual educator can do. This emphasis is important because teachers, administrators, and staff have the power to promote human potential—even when faced with bureaucratic processes, apathetic colleagues, hostile students, inadequate facilities, poorly designed programs, and reactionary policies. The educator facing such negative forces can still be a profoundly beneficial presence in the lives of oneself and others. Accomplishing this is much more enjoyable and is more likely to occur when everybody and everything in and around schools are working together. The last two chapters of *Inviting School Success* describe inviting school cultures and suggest systematic ways to develop them.

It is not the purpose of this book to examine at length total quality management policies, instructional programs, or physical plants. Yet clear evidence exists, as presented by Brubaker (1994), Lezotte (1990), and others, that these factors—reflected in the quality of life found in and around schools—have a significant relationship to student self-esteem and student achievement.

Traditionally, the quality of educational plants, programs, and policies have been treated as variables important primarily for their relationship to student achievement. However, a number of researchers (Amos, 1985; Beane, 1990; Gerber, 1982) have looked at student satisfaction as a separate, important outcome of schooling in its own right. Demeaning, humiliating, or denying the rights of students may be judged wrong despite any evidence that these actions result in desired outcomes.

People, and the places, policies, programs, and processes they create and maintain, may be judged wrongly in spite of accomplishments. From the invitational education perspective, the school athletic team is wrong when it buys success by deliberately holding young boys back a year in school so they will be stronger and more mature on the athletic field. The marching band is wrong when it prides itself with its trophies, but dissuades many young people from music. The school is wrong when it brags about its SAT scores, but ignores its high drop-out rate. The teacher is wrong when he or she maintains "good" discipline through corporal punishment or psychological terrorism. The ends do *not* justify the means.

Inviting schools are places where people enjoy teaching and learning and where policies, programs, and processes contribute to this joy. Student and teacher connectedness and fulfillment not only lead to academic achievement, but are also legitimate goals in and of themselves. As Sergiovanni (1994) pointed out, these wider-ranging fulfillment goals should be based on a different metaphor for schools, one that looks at schools as communities rather than organizations.

This chapter presents a metaphor of what the authors consider to be an inviting school. Two models are presented: the *efficient factory* and the *inviting family.* Preference for one over the other greatly influences the total quality of life in schools. Both models are not so much discrete entities as two aspects of a continuum.

Unfortunately, North American education has moved too close to the efficient factory model. By presenting and arguing for an inviting family metaphor for schools, invitational education seeks to lessen the dominance of the factory model and to provide a more appropriate alternative based on human striving for connectedness and fulfillment.

The Efficient Factory

Many differences exist among factories, but traditionally most factories have placed emphasis on the following six characteristics: (1) mass production, (2) uniform product, (3) cost effectiveness, (4) technology, (5) centralized control, and (6) workers as functionaries. It will be useful to consider these characteristics in turn.

Mass Production

In the efficient factory, a large number of units, all alike, are turned out by assembly lines. In some cases, depending on a marketing analysis and the promotional activities of the sales department, minor differences in appearance and performance are introduced. But these differences are in various models and not in individual units coming off the line. The major emphasis is on quantity. Raw materials are graded, hammered, shaped, processed, conditioned, and turned into a standard and uniform product.

Uniform Product

The efficient factory is supervised closely to ensure that each product meets minimum standards of quality and sameness. The process requires many experts who are charged with ensuring quality control. These experts monitor, sample, test, and approve or reject goods. Products that are damaged in the factory process, or that differ in any significant way, are rejected and shoved aside. These rejects will later be recycled, destroyed, or marked down and sold at discount as irregulars, odd lots, close-outs, or seconds, often without brand name or identification. These inferior goods, sometimes found in factory outlets, damaged goods stores, discount houses, or flea markets, failed to meet the minimum required standards of uniformity.

Cost Effectiveness

In the efficient factory, the highest priority is cost effectiveness. The aesthetics of the plant are relatively unimportant. Factories are designed without windows to control the climate, reduce maintenance, and prevent vandalism and theft. Efficient factories are often surrounded by chain-link fences topped with barbed wire and have gates and guards on duty around the clock. Cost corners are cut wherever possible, and short-term profits are sometimes given priority over long-range planning. In almost every policy decision, costs are the bottom line.

Technology

Technological advances are greatly valued in the efficient factory and are introduced into plants as quickly as possible. Considerable attention is paid to such hardware items as computers, automatic equipment, pro-grammed delivery systems, and other inventions designed to provide swift and sure processing procedures. Even workers are seen as physical objects to be combined with the latest machinery to provide still more technological efficiency.

Centralized Control

In the efficient factory, planning is usually separated from production. Authority flows from the top down, from board to executives, to produc-tion managers, to plant superintendents, to supervisors, and finally to workers. Policies and programs are traditionally developed in places and by people far removed from the production line in function and status, if not in distance. Managers and workers have their respective functions and prerogatives, and workers have little voice in planning. Workers get what they can by organizing, bargaining, and when necessary by striking.

But whatever workers get, it usually does not include a role in policy formulation of program design. This formulation is done by boards of directors, executive management, and design experts.

Workers as Functionaries

Workers in the efficient factory are expected to be punctual, obedient, conforming, and above all *busy.* Individual needs, interests, and personalities are relatively unimportant. Work is broken into small, easy to understand, mistake-proof tasks. The workers are controlled by clocks, bells, buzzers, whistles, shifts, public address systems, assembly lines, and a host of supervisors. Efficiency studies are made regularly to monitor the entire process to ensure maximum production. Meanwhile, public relations departments project the image of the happy worker.

These efficient factory characteristics are certainly not comprehensive or universal, but they do suggest the organizational nature of the traditional industrial plant. Such organization has produced an avalanche of material goods, much of it good and some of it shoddy. In return for the cornucopia of products, the world has paid a heavy price in human suffering and discontent and environmental pollution and destruction.

Now let's look at how the efficient factory model has been adopted in schools.

The Efficient Factory School

The six factory characteristics described previously have their counterparts in schools.

Mass Production

The sheer size of schools has been increased so that some now enroll students by the thousands. As in the efficient factory, quantity takes precedence over quality, and minimal standards take priority over optimal goals. Curricula are established and requirements are made to ensure that all students take certain subjects and get certain basic material in a mass lock-step procedure based on outcome variables.

Uniform Product

Never before in North American education has such emphasis been placed on uniform product. Testing experts are everywhere, and *quality control, performance indicators, curriculum alignment, exit skills, behavioral objectives, outcome measures, minimal competencies,* and *standardized test scores* have entered the language. Uniform productivity is ensured by "mandated" pupil achievement, minimal competency tests, exit skills at each learning station, and frequent performance testing on "objective" multiple choice tests.

Nonconforming students are recycled by being made to repeat grades. If they do manage to make it through high school, students who do not meet minimum academic standards may be given a certificate of attendance rather than a high school diploma. Other nonconforming students may be shunted off to alternative schools or ejected totally from the learning environment, as suspensions and expulsions.

Cost Effectiveness

Like efficient factories, many schools make cost effectiveness the highest priority. Aesthetic considerations are relatively unimportant. Schools are designed without windows to save heat, reduce maintenance, and prevent vandalism. Frills are kept to a minimum or eliminated completely, along with programs such as art, drama and music that do not "pay" their own way in terms of improving standardized test scores. Educational policies are made based on cost effectiveness, and only those programs that are cost effective survive.

Technology

North American education is a major world market for hardware and software designed to instruct students more efficiently and effectively. This is particularly true in the efficient factory school. Early on, students are introduced to instructional centers and learning labs that boast technological advances such as interactive television, talking microcomputers, touch-screen systems, speech-recognition software, fiber-optic listening stations, audiovisual packages, multimedia computers, and CD-ROM. Teachers and students are surrounded by kits, units, modules, sets, packs, printers, programs, and other expensive devices (Wright, 1993).

Teachers are encouraged to instruct through the use of "teacher-proof," packaged, highly-structured programs. At every turn, technological developments influence, and in many cases dictate, the educational process (Postman, 1993).

Centralized Control

Superintendents, school boards, state departments of education, and even the federal government mandate standards for students, teachers, and other persons who work in schools. This standardizing process is supported in the efficient factory school as a necessary part of the organizational structure. Professional relationships are hierarchical, with a flow of authority from the top down, from school board to superintendent, to principal or supervisor, to teacher, and then to students. As is typically the case with remote administrative authority, a wide gulf usually exists between the *mandators* and the *mandated*.

Workers as Functionaries

In the efficient factory school, teachers and students have relatively little control over their workaday lives. Entries and exits are controlled by schedules and punctuated by bells. What is to be taught and learned, as well as why, how, when, and to or by whom, is determined by textbook writers, accrediting agencies, state department officials, directors of curriculum, university consultants, or active pressure groups (Apple, 1987). Learning is defined in terms of basic skill mastery, performance on standardized tests, or learning outcomes designed by people far removed from the classroom. Teachers are interchangeable. They are expected to be docile, hard-working, and responsive to the system's needs. Students are expected to fit into the system, and pupil purposes are generally ignored.

Keeping the foregoing six characteristics of the efficient factory model in mind, turn to another metaphor, that of the inviting family.

The Inviting Family

As mentioned in Chapter One, the word *invitation* comes from the Latin *invitare* which means "to summon cordially, not to shun." This meaning is essential to positive family relationships, in which each family member is summoned to realize his or her unique potential and no one in the family is shunned. The inviting family does not have any standardized form, however, it does have six basic characteristics: (1) respect for individual uniqueness, (2) cooperative spirit, (3) sense of belonging, (4) pleasing habitat, (5) positive expectations, and (6) vital connections to society. Let's examine these six characteristics.

Respect for Individual Uniqueness

The inviting family appreciates individual differences. Not everyone is expected to be alike or to do the same thing. Family members who are unable or unwilling to meet traditional expectations or aspirations are tolerated. "He's not heavy, he's my brother" reflects this attitude of support. There is also a great and shared pride in those who exceed the family's fondest hopes. Flexible and varied living arrangements are promoted as each family member moves toward his or her own creative ways of being. In the inviting family, the concept of *each is unique and has something to offer* determines family policy.

Cooperative Spirit

"One for all and all for one" describes the inviting family. Adults and children learn from each other. The family is seen by all its members as a cooperative enterprise in which cooperation is valued over competition. When one member achieves, all members feel a part of the success. And when one member is having difficulty, it is a family concern. Everyone pitches in to help until the person is able to more adequately participate. In the inviting family, a special watch is kept for those in the family who might need a special boost. This support is always provided within a circle of unconditional respect for the feelings of those who may need assistance.

Sense of Belonging

A most important quality of the inviting family is a deep sense of belonging. This feeling is cultivated wherever possible. Family members spend time talking with each other and sharing their feelings and concerns. They make a special effort to look beyond their own immediate gratification to the needs of other family members. Everyone thinks in terms of *our* family, *our* home, *our* traditions, *our* responsibilities. This loyalty toward one another and the warmth felt for one another result in mutual appreciation, positive self-esteem, and a deep sense of family togetherness.

Pleasing Habitat

Aesthetics are given a high priority in the inviting family. Living green plants, attractive colors, comfortable furniture, soft lighting, open space, cleanliness, pleasant smells, fresh air, and comfortable temperatures are provided wherever possible. Changes in the physical environment are made regularly to keep the habitat attractive. The emphasis on creating an aesthetic environment, even in the most difficult situations, is beautifully illustrated by Betty Smith in her book *A Tree Grows in Brooklyn* (1943), in which a poor family obtains a piano at great effort and personal sacrifice. In the inviting family habitat, everything is designed to send the message: "Be as comfortable as possible, we're glad you're here."

Positive Expectations

Encouraging each family member to realize his or her unique potential is an important quality of the inviting family. Family members expect good things of themselves and others, but these expectations are always presented within an atmosphere of respect. Every effort is made to encourage feelings of self-control and individual responsibility and to encourage members to realize their physical, social, and psychological potential.

Vital Connections to Society

The inviting family is not an insulated container, but a form of continued sustenance for connections to the larger society. Individual family members have wide and various interactions in the world and bring back ideas to share with the rest of the family. There is much excitement and growth in sharing experiences and a respectful treatment for differences of opinion. In addition, family members take into the world the unique insights and skills they have gained from their active participation in family life. The inviting family provides nourishment for individual and societal democratic development.

Now, relate the inviting family to the inviting family school.

The Inviting Family School

The following six characteristics describe the *inviting family school* and parallel the basic qualities of the inviting family.

Respect for Individual Uniqueness

A hallmark of the inviting family school is that judgments and evaluations are made primarily on a personal basis. Each child is seen as *unique* and is treated as such. Where grades are used, every effort is made to ensure that the marking system is used for the welfare of the student involved. If a student's progress falls behind, he or she is placed in "intensive care," just like at-risk patients in hospitals. Students are encouraged to test themselves and judge their own personal performance and progress. Errors are viewed as a source of information rather than as a sign of failure. Further, students participate in making decisions about how grading and evaluation processes will be applied. All students are encouraged to have confidence in their ability to learn, to trust their feelings, and to celebrate their personal uniqueness.

Cooperative Spirit

In the inviting family school, peer teaching is encouraged so that both tutors and tutored may benefit. In every way, people in the school are expected to take cooperative responsibility for what happens in their shared lives. Everyone is expected to participate in the decision-making process. Teachers, students, and adult caregivers are not isolated from decision-making, but rather, in a very real sense, are "executives" of the school. A related feature of the inviting family school is that competition is minimized in favor of mutual support. Students who are unable to achieve as expected are offered extra help—always within a caring, respectful stance. School activities are based on cooperation, collaboration, and mutual concern.

Sense of Belonging

The inviting family school cherishes community warmth and togetherness. Students and teachers think in terms of *our* school, *our* work, and all of *us* together. Students are kept together as much as possible. If one student must be removed from the group, it is for as short a period as possible. Every effort is made to encourage feelings of school pride and of being a member of a learning and caring community. Perhaps this sense of belonging can best be illustrated by one student's high school experience: "Our school is like a big, caring family. When my father died, all my teachers were at the funeral home. My senior class collected money and sent a wreath. I'll never forget their kindness."

Pleasing Habitat

A pleasant environment for living and learning is stressed in the inviting family school. The landscape, upkeep, and general appearance of the school are given careful attention. Teachers, staff, and students take *shared* responsibility with custodians to create and maintain an aesthetically pleasing physical environment. Regardless of the school's age, everyone takes pride in maintaining it as attractively as possible. Extra efforts are made to ensure that lighting, acoustic qualities, temperature, room design, window areas, furniture arrangement, colors, use of space, and displays all contribute to an appealing and comfortable setting.

Positive Expectations

Efforts are made in the inviting family school to encourage positive and realistic student self-concepts. Students are taught that each person has relatively untapped capacities for learning and that this learning is something that happens with their consent and involvement—not something that is done to them. Students participate in deciding what they will study, how much they will learn, how fast they will learn, and how they will evaluate their own individual progress. Each student is encouraged by positive expectations communicated by teachers. These teachers, in turn, have a sense of personal efficacy and high expectations for themselves.

Vital Connections to Society

The inviting family school encourages many and varied democratic interactions between and among members of the school and the community. Older students work with younger students, support staff may coach a sporting team or give some instruction on an area of expertise, community members may assist with a drama production, an outside agency may schedule meetings at the school.

Parent volunteers are seen as vital to school success, and partnerships with local businesses and community organizations are promoted. In addition, students go out into the community, participate in, study, and discuss many of its activities and organizations. Going beyond the local community, larger societal and global issues are discussed in a respectful democratic manner. Students are encouraged to think globally and act locally in applying the concepts they learn in schools. They see their school experiences as a vital base for participating in and bettering society.

Move now from the world of theoretical models to an imaginary visit to an inviting family school.

An Imaginary Visit to an Inviting School

Until now, this chapter has presented two metaphors for twenty-first century schools: efficient factory and inviting family. The acceptance of either model will greatly influence children's lives. The authors of this book vigorously advocate the inviting family metaphor. The following imaginary vignette adds more detail to the proposed model.

Although no two inviting family schools would look alike, there is a certain unmistakable "chemistry" to the school. The following is an extension of a depiction developed earlier (Purkey & Novak, 1988) of what an inviting family school might look like to parents about to register their children in the school.

Picture yourself and your family moving into a strange town. Your big question is, "What are the schools like?" You soon find out. Even before you move you obtain a copy of the town's paper and notice it contains several articles regarding the local schools. The high school choral group is planning a tour of Europe; a student wins a science prize; two teachers are just back from an archaeological dig sponsored by the state university; a counselor has published a book of poetry. A special column titled "About Our Schools" contains a list of upcoming events and activities. You immediately get the feeling that there is energy, pride, and purpose in this community's schools.

When you and your family arrive in your new town, you spend considerable time with a Realtor who is a strong school supporter. She tells you that she recently attended a breakfast reception for the town's Realtors hosted by the high school faculty and staff. The Realtor states how impressed she was with the overall professionalism of the school personnel.

As you find your way around town, you notice that the local bank has student work on display, as do several stores and public buildings. That evening, a special program on a local television station deals with the recent academic successes of the local schools.

When the moving van is unloaded, you call the school to enroll your children. The school phone is answered promptly and courteously; the information you need is provided quickly and efficiently. The person on the phone says how pleased the school will be to have your children as new students. An appointment is scheduled for you and your children to visit the school and complete the enrollment process.

As you drive onto the school grounds to enroll your children you observe numerous, positively worded signs. The first sign you see is "Welcome to our school." Instead of "No Parking," another sign reads, "Please park in designated areas." Instead of "Visitors must report to the principal's office," a third sign reads, "We care for our children and their safety. Please check in at the principal's office." Parking spaces directly in front of the main entrance are marked "Reserved for guests."

Other indications of the inviting school philosophy are everywhere. The grass is mowed, bushes trimmed, flowers planted, walkways clean, and the windows sparkle. Although the building was constructed more than a half-century ago, its physical condition conveys the sense of pride that everyone has in the school.

When you and your children enter the school and approach the principal's office, you smell fresh flowers and notice the green plants, fresh paint, and waxed floors. On entering the principal's outer office, you are promptly greeted by a professionally-dressed school representative who identifies herself, shakes hands with you *and* your children, and says that the school faculty and staff are looking forward to meeting your family. The representative then asks you and your children to be seated in a comfortable reception area while packets of orientation materials are quickly assembled for you. There is no traditional counter in this school office—only a receptionist's desk and comfortable furniture arranged to make you feel like you are in the reception area of a first-class organization that cares about people. A volunteer student guide soon arrives to take you and your children on a tour of the school.

After introducing himself in a friendly and confident manner, the student guide leads you and your family around the school. The first place you visit is a well-furnished and attractively decorated classroom. The guide explains that at least one classroom remains decorated all summer, like a model apartment, to show visitors what the whole building will look like when school begins.

Your student guide then takes you to a beautifully maintained cafeteria featuring a French village theme, with individual tables, awnings, plants, and scenic murals on the walls. The guide mentions that classical music is always played during lunchtime. "If we can't hear the music, we're being too loud," he explains.

Next you visit the teachers' lounge and workroom, where there is a large collection of professional journals, an honor-system lending library, and colorful bulletin boards with both professional and personal notices. Like the rest of the school, the room is clean and the air is fresh. A vending machine offers fruit juices. From the poster and the vending machines, you conclude that this school faculty has an active wellness program in place.

Toward the end of your tour, you stop at a student restroom and notice how clean it is: There are mirrors on the wall and soap and paper-towel dispensers over each sink, no graffiti is seen in the bathroom, and there are doors on the stalls. At the end of your visit, you and your children are escorted to your car and presented with a bumper sticker that reads: "OUR SCHOOLS: THE MOST INVITING PLACES IN TOWN." You are beginning to understand why.

When you arrive home and read the materials in the school information packet, attractively printed in the school colors, you learn that both the curricular and cocurricular activities call for a high level of student and teacher involvement. The simply worded statement on school policies reflects unconditional respect for everyone in the school. The few rules are reasonable and enforceable. Most important, there is a genuine commitment to every student in the school.

The next day you receive a letter from the school thanking you for your visit and explaining that you will soon be contacted by members of volunteer groups that are part of the school family. These groups, from band boosters to room sponsors, from gardening clubs to older adult clubs, work in and around the school. They will be inviting your entire family to participate in the life of the school. As you settle in your new home, you have good feelings regarding your choice of this town, its outstanding school system, and the welfare of your children.

Summary

Metaphors do matter. They provide a way of focusing attention and making sense of complex situations. This chapter suggested that looking at schools as either efficient factories or inviting families results in different qualities being emphasized and different ways of doing things defended. The imaginary summer visit to an inviting school provided a clear instance of the philosophy expressed in this book. The next chapter looks at how a school can systematically embody this approach.

8

Creating Inviting
Schools

*Leaders articulate and define what has previously remained
implicit or unsaid; then they invent images, metaphors, and models
that provide a focus for new attention.*

Warren Bennis and Burt Nanus,
Leaders: The Strategies for Taking Charge (1985, p. 39)

When it comes to creating inviting schools, there is good news and bad
news. First the bad news: There is no magic formula for creating inviting
schools because each school, like each family, has its own unique characteristics. To impose a standard form on all schools would be to miss
the living qualities that make each school unique. Now the good news:
Some schools (Blackburn, 1990; Chance, 1990, 1992; Purkey, Strahan,
Corders & Lucas, 1994), school systems (Bennedict, 1990; McBrien,
1990), and universities (Lehr, 1990; Stehle, 1990; Wilson, 1990) have
successfully implemented invitational education programs. From an
analysis of these and other experiences, a cumulative 12-step plan of
action for creating inviting schools, called HELIX, has been developed
(Purkey & Novak, 1993).

The Invitational HELIX

Creating an inviting school involves an awareness and understanding of the theory presented in this book, applying this theory to real situations, and a commitment by those involved to work together to realize shared goals. Coordinating these efforts on a schoolwide basis requires making sense of many different parts and understanding how each part works progressively to create an intentionally inviting school.

This chapter introduces a guidance system, called HELIX (Purkey & Novak, 1993) that was developed in response to calls for more complex analyses of invitational education (Stillion & Siegel, 1985) and for greater emphasis on the deeper ethical and democratic implications of the inviting process (Novak, 1992b). HELIX is a practical guide for educators seeking to make their school "the most inviting place in town."

HELIX is based on the idea that for educators to use invitational education they have to move from being aware of it, to understanding it, to applying it, and finally to being committed to adopting it and keeping it going. Thus, adopting invitational education involves four stages: awareness, understanding, application, and adoption. In addition, schools can be at different phases in employing invitational education. Some schools may be merely seeking to introduce some inviting practices; others may wish to apply invitational education in a systematic way. Still others wish to have it as their pervasive philosophy. With this progression of purposes in mind, three phases have been identified: occasional, systematic, and pervasive, depending on the school's degree of commitment. HELIX spirals through four stages while progressing through three phases. HELIX's 12-step guide enables practitioners to identify at what stage and phase their school is presently functioning and what is the next higher step in becoming an inviting school.

Although a plethora of bandwagons for educational change seem to exist, most do not get at the deep structures of schools (Fullan, 1991). Using HELIX is a way to build on invitational education's intuitive appeal and take it to progressively higher phases. Let's look at each phase and step of HELIX, which is a diagram designed to illustrate the process of creating an inviting school.

Figure 8-1. The Invitational HELIX

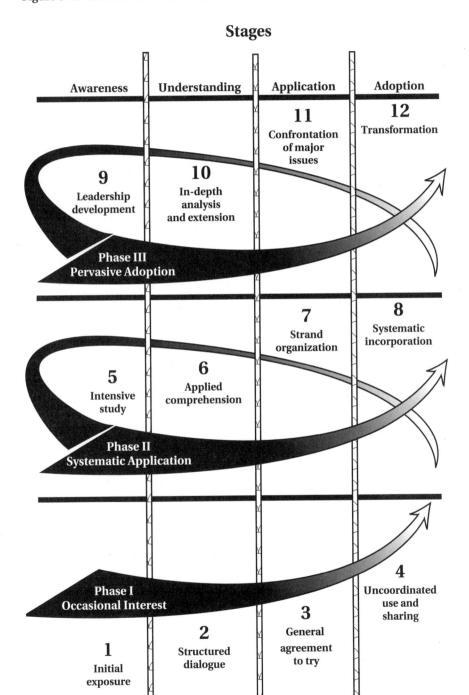

Occasional Interest (Phase I)

All schools are inviting in some ways at some times. The beginning phase of HELIX aims at helping people in a school recognize and sustain current practices that are inviting and try out some new ways of doing things. This initial phase provides beginning level exposure to invitational education, encourages some awareness of its terminology, and identifies ways to introduce inviting practices within the school. What marks this phase as the beginning level is that it is characterized by a variety of suggestions that are only tangentially related. The suggestions often provide affirmation for methods and skills already in practice in the school. These suggestions are nonthreatening, generally unrelated to each other, and relatively easy to apply.

Phase I processes are concerned with creating an inviting ambiance within the school, which might include changing signs on buildings, hanging plants in the foyer, painting stairwells, answering telephones differently, or organizing social events. Although positive, these introductory activities bring about little change in the deep structure of the school. They are, however, important in themselves and prepare the school for higher levels of inviting.

Initial Exposure (Step 1)

This first step deals with a beginning awareness of invitational education. This initial exposure might take place while educators are attending a conference or workshop, hearing a speaker, reading an article or book (such as this one), talking with colleagues, or viewing a videotape. Ideally, this dawning of awareness is an enjoyable experience that prepares educators for the interactions necessary for the next step.

Structured Dialogue (Step 2)

Good ideas gain additional meaning when they are shared. This second step involves some form of organized discussion within the school. This might be an afternoon meeting following a morning general session program, a retreat, a series of team or job-alike meetings, or other type of organized discussion on ways to apply invitational education within the school. Although the emphasis at this step is on better understanding the inviting approach, this understanding is enhanced by recognizing and appreciating practices already taking place in the school that are clearly inviting. Participants in the dialogue at this step can explain *why* certain practices are inviting or disinviting.

General Agreement to Try (Step 3)

This next step takes people from structured dialogue to a general consensus among school members to try various inviting ideas and suggestions. This is still the beginning phase, so these trials typically consist of uncoordinated individual or small-group efforts. The purpose of Step 3 is to try out new ideas and see what works. Guskey (1986) and Schommer (1990) reported that a discussion of what works is very important for incorporating new practices and beliefs into daily practice. In this step, small modifications and innovations, such as making signs more positively worded, improving the lighting at work stations, or sending appreciation cards are expected and welcome.

Uncoordinated Use and Sharing (Step 4)

The beginning phase of HELIX concludes by adopting various suggestions to make the school more inviting. People in the school incorporate the ideas they have experimented with in the previous step. These practices remain largely unorganized and uncoordinated, yet they become a part of everyday school practice. Because they work well and are occasionally publicly recognized, they are likely to be a permanent part of the school culture. It is important to recognize these successes, both within the school and beyond. Recognizing successes prepares the ground for advanced levels of practice.

Systematic Application (Phase II)

After people in a school have heard about, discussed, tried, and successfully applied some inviting practices, they then develop relationships among these various practices to produce integrative change within the school. Integrative change means that people are willing to work together to systematically affect practices in the whole school. Educators look beyond their own classrooms, their own offices, and their own students to try to develop a mutually satisfiable way to make the school operation a shared enterprise.

The sense that "we are in this together" takes hold during the systematic application phase as people look at the school as a whole and work in groups to develop inviting places, policies, programs, and processes. In this phase also, students, parents, and members of the community are encouraged to become involved in examining, proposing, implementing, and evaluating suggestions for improvement. For these systematic activities to work, members of the school seek to create an atmosphere that manifests trust, intentionality, respect, and optimism.

Intensive Study (Step 5)

Because educators are now seeking to apply invitational education in a systematic way, they need an awareness of invitational education as a system. And so this step is characterized by systematic study of invitational education. School members need to become aware of the various components of the invitational model, including its foundations, assumptions, areas, levels, and choices. This systematic study should be directed by an experienced and knowledgeable person who has a sound background in, and commitment to, invitational education. Step 5 requires careful reading and usually involves a full-day intensive workshop and follow-up.

Applied Comprehension (Step 6)

Understanding invitational education as an integrated plan of action requires time to set in and be discussed. At this step those involved make efforts to explain their understanding of invitational education, to reflect on what is presently happening in the school, and to compare what is taking place in light of what is desirable.

Strand Organization (Step 7)

This step introduces the "5 P's" approach to implementing invitational education by creating five "strands" (teams of people) within the school. Each strand takes one of the five P's (People, Places, Policies, Programs, and Processes) as a home base. A rotation method is then used so that all strands will have input into each strand's goals, procedures, obstacles, overcoming obstacles, and evaluation. At Step 7, a coordinator for each strand is appointed and general consensus is reached with the strand members about the priority of the goals to be pursued.

Systematic Incorporation (Step 8)

With the strands working as operational units (often with their own name and logo), the goal ofthis step is to institutionalize the 5 P's strands and their work throughout the school. This involves regular strand meetings, coordinator meetings, feedback to all members of the school, and special efforts to keep things going. In addition, networks may be formed with other schools and organizations and plans made for long-term staff development. By the conclusion of this step, the school has made significant progress toward developing an inviting culture.

Pervasive Adoption (Phase III)

Schools are complex organizations in which many things are tried, but only a select few are retained to become part of the operating culture. The goal of Phase III is to have invitational education pervade the entire fabric of the school. In other words, invitational education becomes internalized in the institutional norms and "the way things are done here" (Fink, 1992). This requires sustained dialogue about the assumptions of invitational education and the continued development of a community where democratic leadership flourishes. The school becomes a place where everyone works together so that "what's good gets done" (Sergiovanni, 1992, 1994). As a result of this participation, a school will have many leaders who can use invitational education as a creative and sustained heuristic to examine and deal with issues of personal, professional, institutional, and societal importance.

Not only are members of the school community congenial and civil, they are also collegial. They respect each other's intentions and competence, and they make concerted efforts to learn from, and with, one another. Members of this learning community become invitational leaders and their schools are seen as exemplary models of invitational education. These individuals and schools take a proactive stance that incorporates, explores, and extends the deepest intellectual and ethical commitments of the inviting perspective.

Leadership Development (Step 9)

Chapter One explained that invitational education is a developing theory of practice, with avenues unexplored and questions unanswered. During this step, educators become leaders in invitational education by exploring difficult issues and constructing new practices. Discussions at this step take place formally and informally, within and outside of school.

Formally, at regularly scheduled school meetings and committee strand sessions, participants seek connections between invitational education and other school goals. This may result in developing or reconceptualizing the school's mission statement.

Informally, participants share ideas about the inviting approach and extend each other's thinking and practice. This informal networking may result in an awareness of larger networks of kindred spirits and an understanding of invitational education's relationship to other educational programs. Step 9 also provides an excellent opportunity for experienced practitioners of invitational education to refresh their practice and develop additional inviting approaches to teaching, learning, and living.

In-Depth Analysis and Extension (Step 10)

Leaders in invitational education are asked to critically analyze invitational education and to compare and contrast it with other educational systems and approaches. They can look at other educational programs and evaluate them according to five questions (The first four were developed by Purkey and Schmidt [1995]):

- Is there a perceptual orientation?
- Is there an emphasis on an educationally developed self-concept?
- Is the approach humanely effective?
- Does the approach encourage applicability?
- Does the approach develop democratic deliberation?

Answering these questions enables practitioners of invitational education to be both prudent and constructive. With a conceptual and ethical anchorage, educators can avoid jumping on questionable educational bandwagons while incorporating positive aspects of other approaches. They can evaluate texts on invitational education (Novak, 1991) and work on collaborative efforts to modify the theory (Novak, 1992a). At this step, practitioners of invitational education can explain it in multiple ways to varied audiences. (A key test to check on this ability is to explain invitational education without using the word "inviting.")

Confrontation of Major Challenges (Step 11)

Advanced understanding of invitational education can begin with reflective insight, but it culminates in creative application. Participants in this step of HELIX can take a proactive stance toward challenges that are facing their school and society. Thus, they can address, in a civil way, basic issues regarding the symbolic webbing of their school. They ask and honestly seek answers to such questions as these:

- What is our school really about?
- Is our school doing what it should be doing?
- Are we reaching all the students in our school?
- Are there some school or societal policies, programs, or processes that are unfair or insensitive to certain races, sexes, ethnic, or socio-economic groups?
- What can we do to prepare students to help develop a more democratic society?

Developing answers to these questions leads to creating more inviting school practices and a socially integrating sense of purpose as identified by Tyack and Hansot (1982). An important process here is to use student, parent, and community insights and participation to help make this sense of purpose take hold.

Transformation (Step 12)

By this step, invitational theory is rooted in every aspect of life in and around the school. It is reflected in people's interactions, the school's outside and inside appearance, the programs established, the policies supported, and the processes that are followed. The school acts as an inviting family in that it consistently demonstrates respect for individual uniqueness, cooperative spirit, sense of belonging, pleasing habitat, positive expectations, and vital connections to society.

Individuals and school teams are asked to present programs at meetings and conferences to describe how and why their school works—and they do this with enthusiasm, grace, and skill. Their school is seen as a model for what education can become. School community members have learned the creative merger of the possible and the imaginative in handling conflict and in developing principled plans of action. Their school is filled with hope as they continually seek ways to put into practice the assumptions of invitational education:

- People are able, valuable, and responsible and should be treated accordingly.

- Schools should be cooperative and integrative.

- Process is as important as product.

- People possess untapped potential in all areas of worthwhile human endeavor.

- Human potential can best be realized by places, policies, programs, and processes specifically designed to invite development, and by people who are intentionally inviting with themselves and others, personally and professionally.

Invitational education can have a positive, sustained, and creative impact on school cultures. HELIX was developed with this in mind to guide spokespersons who have an awareness of the deep commitments involved in the theory; possess a sound and expanding understanding of its parts and whole; apply imaginatively and courageously its techniques and spirit; and use skill and persistence to develop within their schools an inviting culture and connections to a more democratic society. This requires deep commitments, solid thinking, and coordinated actions.

As Michael Fullan (1991) pointed out, the process of change is not usually some sequential, step-by-step approach. Many factors enter into the change equation and often, at best, it is two steps forward and one step back. HELIX is not a magic formula that can change this; however, HELIX can engender discussion and offer suggestions regarding future steps. Using HELIX to start a dialogue about where a school should be going can be a way to get a school unstuck. HELIX is based on hope for positive change. Creating inviting schools is fundamentally an imaginative act of hope. Here is an example of a school that systematically put invitational education to work to change the school culture.

Invitational Education at Work

In 1990, several indicators suggested that the morale among faculty, staff, students, and parents at Douglas Byrd Junior High School were bending under the strain of trying to meet the needs of a large and challenging student body. As explained in the opening to this book, the very high dropout and absentee rates at Byrd, coupled with very low standardized test scores, made Byrd a great testing ground for invitational education.

Although many efforts had been made to improve teaching and create a positive climate for learning, Byrd educators expressed growing frustration and burnout with the proportion of time spent on crisis intervention. For example, the faculty absenteeism rate was the highest of any school in the county. A few parents and community volunteers assisted with the tutoring programs, but they too felt overwhelmed by the magnitude of the need.

In writing a proposal for outside funding through the RJR Nabisco Next-Century-Schools Project, Byrd educators and volunteers developed STAR—**S**tudents **T**ogether **A**chieving **R**ecognition. STAR's goal was to create an educational environment that would enhance the abilities, strengths, and worth of everyone in the life of Douglas Byrd Junior High School. Several faculty members were familiar with invitational education and, after much reading and discussion, invitational education was selected as the best model for Douglas Byrd.

When Byrd Junior High was selected to become one of RJR Nabisco's Next-Century-Schools, Byrd teachers and administrators began a series of meetings with the authors of this book and other leaders in invitational education to plan a systematic approach for introducing the model at Byrd. Everyone involved in this planning agreed from the beginning that the intent was not merely to reorganize services or restructure education at Byrd, but rather to truly transform the quality of life in school for everyone involved.

The 5 P's of invitational education provided the vehicle for transforming Douglas Byrd. The 5 P's include the *people* who were encouraged to be intentionally inviting with themselves and others, personally and professionally, and the *places, policies, programs,* and *processes* specifically designed to invite development. These five powerful P's addressed the school's global nature and were designed to transform the educative process by applying steady and continuous pressure from a number of points.

The Implementation Process

The plan to implement invitational education at Byrd was to offer a special "Opening of School Celebration" that had some unusual features, an intensive leadership training program, and an ongoing series of inservice workshops.

At the Opening of School Celebration, teachers, administrators, representative students, and parents gathered at a Fayetteville hotel for a day-long celebration of promises and plans for the future. After a general session that presented the basic concepts of invitational education, participants were divided into five "strand" sessions organized by the P's of invitational education (People, Places, Policies, Programs, and Processes). Discussion in the five strand sessions focused on three areas: current strengths, shared concerns, and suggestions for transformation. Strands began working through the GOALS process to maximize the involvement (**G**oal setting, **O**utlining actions, **A**nticipating obstacles, **L**isting Alternatives and **S**pecifying action plans). Strand leaders were identified to coordinate meetings throughout the school year. All of these activities were coordinated by a GOALS committee, and all were built around invitational education. Each strand group developed its own focus and style. Here is a brief summary of what each strand did:

People: To revitalize the quality of life for everyone at Douglas Byrd, individuals were encouraged to ask what could be done to nurture relationships in ways that intentionally reflect trust, respect, and optimism.

Places: The group asked this question: "Is Douglas Byrd a pleasant, aesthetic, clean, and functional place where people want to be and want to learn?" All facilities and grounds were examined, and ways were found to enhance the physical environment of Byrd.

Policies: In reviewing policies at Byrd, ways were sought to ensure that all rules, regulations, and requirements were inclusive, positive, encouraging, and involving. Policies were seen as a critical part of the chemistry that determines the spirit of Byrd.

Programs: All programs at Byrd were reviewed to ensure they worked for the general welfare of the school. Those programs that appeared to be ethnocentric, elitist, sexist, or discriminating were modified or eliminated.

Processes: Finally, the processes employed to transform Byrd were themselves evaluated. How a more exciting, satisfying, and enriching school is created is as important as what is created. At Byrd, everyone had a voice in deciding how things would be done democratically.

During the project's three years, leadership training sessions with teachers, parents, staff, and administration provided opportunities to discuss and coordinate the invitational education model. Action plans were circulated, and priorities established across the strands. Inservice sessions were conducted to facilitate strand goals. Strand groups began meeting to address specific needs, Among the many workshops were sessions on cultural diversity, conflict management, classroom discipline, cooperative learning, teaming, advisor and advisee activities, and student evaluation. In every session, invitational education provided an organizing theory, a practical model, and a common language for school transformation.

What Was Accomplished?

Here are some changes recorded from year one (1989 to 1990) to year three (1992 to 1993) of the project.

People
- Recognition of teachers increased from 10 activities to 26.
- Parent/community volunteer hours increased from 1,344 hours to 3,590 hours.
- Students were strongly encouraged to stay in school, and the number of dropouts decreased from 48 to 14.
- Student self-concept-as-learner remained constant over the three-year project and did not decline. (Earlier studies report a lowering of self-concept as students move through the grades.)

Places

- The number of school beautification projects increased 4 to 8.

- The library was given special attention, and average daily circulation of library materials increased from 328 to 365, in spite of a decline in student enrollment.

- The common areas were renovated, chain-link fences removed, and comfortable spaces were developed for students and faculty to congregate. Signs were changed to make them more user-friendly. For example, the "cafeteria" became the "dining room," and "Welcome to Douglas Byrd Junior High School" is the first sign visitors see as they enter Byrd.

Policies

- The number of students retained at grade level decreased from 144 to 110.

- The percentage of D and E grades decreased by 8 percent over the three years.

Programs

- Training sessions resulted in developing cooperative learning projects and interdisciplinary teams: from none to 4.

- Community and school business partnerships increased from 14 to 44.

- Student scores on End of Course testing improved in 4 of 6 basic areas.

Processes

- Total staff development hours increased from 220 hours to almost 5,000 hours.

- The number of academic teams in place and functioning increased from none to 8.

Evidence from evaluations (Stanley, 1993) indicate that many strand goals were met and exceeded. Student and teacher attendance improved. Parent participation in school activities dramatically increased. New workrooms were opened, the physical plant was significantly improved, and a number of beautification projects completed. New partnerships with civic groups were arranged, and participation in tutoring programs increased. Students have been recognized in assemblies and in the local newspaper for a wide variety of achievements. Assemblies built around appreciation for cultural diversity were highly acclaimed by everyone. Teachers have formed interdisciplinary teams and have developed a range of cooperative learning activities and advisor/advisee programs.

By almost any measure, invitational education has transformed Byrd. The number of dropouts has steadily decreased, from 4.2 percent in 1990–1991 to 1.2 percent in 1992–93. Fewer students have received failing grades, and fewer students were retained. The percentage of students earning good grades (A's and B's) has risen steadily, especially among minority students. Evaluations on several formal assessments of school climate have improved (Stanley, 1993). Perceptions of participants as measured by the *Wayson School Climate and Context Inventory* show sustained improvement in all eight dimensions since the fall of 1989.

Perhaps most significantly, teachers and students at Byrd Junior High have come to believe that Byrd is "their school." Participation in the strand teams and tangible evidence of school transformation have begun to alter the symbolic structure of the school, to affect the ways people talk and write and think about their work. Visiting the school on a regular basis, hearing students speak with great pride about their school, seeing their enthusiasm in celebrating successes, watching fences come down and banners go up convinced us that meaningful changes have taken place, with more underway.

What About the Future?

Plans for the future are underway and will focus on "invitational teaching, learning, and living." Teachers are developing more intensive procedures for interdisciplinary teaming, student advisory groups, and integrated instruction. Special programs are in place to ensure the safety of everyone in the school. Now that procedures for planning and coordinating improvements have been established, teachers and administrators are optimistic about the prospects for even more successes. In fact, RJR Nabisco has provided funding for implementing invitational education in a second junior high school in Fayetteville, North Carolina, under a demonstration/dissemination grant.

Within the invitational education framework, school transformation is seen as an ongoing and often fragile process. Although the outcomes of this process are measurable, the changes that matter most are often intangible. The authors' experiences at Byrd Junior High and other schools have helped them to understand more about these intangibles. The changes that have mattered most are those that affect how teachers and students see themselves, each other, and their schools. As students and teachers develop more positive views, the momentum of invitational education grows, and the deep structures that shape school cultures begin to change. Over time, schools become less like factories and more like families: where people want to spend their time and where everyone is summoned cordially to realize their relatively boundless potential in all areas of worthwhile human endeavor.

Conclusion

This book has explored the process of inviting school success. By focusing on the subtle, but pervasive messages extended in the school environment, *Inviting School Success* has emphasized something familiar that has heretofore been overlooked. "You cannot miss the road to the City of Emerald," said the witch in *The Wizard of Oz*, "for it is paved with yellow brick." But Emerald Cities, like invitations in schools, can sometimes be too obvious to see.

Four unhappy characters went to find the Wizard of Oz: a scarecrow who thought he had no brain, a tin woodsman who thought he had no heart, a lion who believed he had no courage, and a young girl who thought she lacked the power to make changes in her life. All were under the delusion that if they could only reach the Great and Terrible Oz, he would grant them the things they lacked. Little did they realize that they already possessed the very things they sought. When the four finally accomplished what they believed they could never do—kill the Wicked Witch of the West—they returned to the Emerald City impatient for their rewards. There they discovered that wizards (like educators) have no magic power.

Yet, the wizard did manage to do things "that everybody knows can't be done." He cared about people, and to each of the four he sent a most powerful invitation: "A testimonial! A decree!" He invited them to see things in themselves that they had overlooked and to use what they already possessed. The lion represents *respect*, the scarecrow represents *optimism*, the tinman represents *trust*, and Dorothy represents *intentionality*. As Dorothy said when she finally got back to Kansas: "Oh, Aunty Em, I've been to many strange and marvelous places looking for something that was right here all along . . . right in my own backyard!"

So it is with inviting school success.

A

Practical Suggestions for the Whole School

There are as many practical ways to invite school success as there are people in and around schools who have imagination and who *want* to invite themselves and others to realize their potential. The following lists contain more than two hundred suggestions that are only examples of these ways. For a much longer list, please consult *The Inviting School Treasury* (Purkey & Stanley, 1994). Consider and choose those that fit your style and your situation. Any group of professionals can come together and create suggestion lists as good or better than these.

The focus of *Inviting School Success* is on the classroom teacher, but everything in schools is connected to everything else. The way the school bus driver treats a student affects how well that student does in class. The manner in which the food is prepared and served in the cafeteria influences what role the principal will play that day. Because of these countless interrelationships, the following lists have been divided into categories illustrating what the elementary school teacher, the food-service professional, the library media specialist, the middle school teacher, the physical educator, the school administrator, the school bus driver, the school counselor, the school secretary, and the secondary-school teacher can do to make schools more inviting places for people.

These lists are dedicated to the single, isolated educator who is determined to make school more inviting. They offer a good beginning to answering the question this educator may be asked by fellow professionals: "Where might I begin to help make our school the most inviting place in town?"

What Elementary School Teachers Can Do

1 *Build momentum*. Before school begins, when you first receive your class roster, send a postcard to each of your incoming students. A brief note, letting each child know that you are looking forward to the pleasure of his or her company, is a fine way to start the school year.

2 *Hold a "young-parent tea party."* Parents who are sending a child to school for the first time often have fears and anxieties about "losing" their children. It can be most helpful if these parents are invited to tea and shown what their children will experience. This is also an excellent way to recruit volunteers for parent aides.

3 *Give an apple on opening day.* We've all heard of an apple for the teacher. Well, switch things around, and on opening day of school have an apple on the desk of each student in your class. This can be a specific way of saying: "How glad I am to have you here, and how much we will learn together this year."

4 *Get off to a fast start.* Children come to school the first day very excited, expecting to learn to read and write. Don't disappoint them. Duplicate a very simple, brief paragraph story with several blanks. "I go to _____ school. My teacher's name is_____." Write the answers on the board and practice. Students can take their papers home and exclaim: "Look what I learned to read and write today!" You are off to a great start.

5 *Take turns reading.* When students take turns reading aloud, the teacher can speed things up, and add to the excitement, by reading aloud after each student. This keeps the pace fast and avoids boredom.

6 *Make individual chalkboards.* Cut pressed wood, masonite board, or similar material and paint with blackboard paint. Each child works on his or her own board, then holds the board up for the teacher to check silently. This results in a private communication between student and teacher, for no one can read another board without turning (unless the seating is arranged in a circle or other nontraditional design).

7 *Build a loft.* Children love snug places, and few places are as comfortable as a loft built across one end of the classroom. (Groups of parents can help with construction.) A loft gives more classroom space, makes a fine corner for small group meetings, a time-out area, or even plays. Sometimes, carpet companies will donate remnants for covering the floor and steps.

8 *Be positive.* Too often directions are negative: "Don't talk," "Stay seated," "Stop running," "Quit that." Try making directions positive by focusing on what should be done, rather than on what should not be done.

9 *Raid the clothes closet.* To help break the ice with a group of students, ask each to bring to class (or wear if appropriate) a favorite article of clothing. Ask each participant to explain how this particular article became a favorite. You will find there is a story in every closet.

10 *Rotate the seating.* When working with smaller children, it helps to rotate the seating from time to time so that each child has the opportunity to sit close to the teacher. This also helps to equalize psychological distance.

11 *Arrange a "down-time" corner.* An overstuffed armchair, a rocking chair, or even an old bathtub piled with pillows, along with a rug, books, and a game or two, can be just the thing to help a student overcome anxieties or anger stemming from some temporary crisis in his or her life.

12 *Lay a class carpet.* Ask each student to bring in one or two pieces of carpet squares. The class can arrange the squares according to their own creativity. The squares can then be fastened to the floor. The carpet will cut down noise, make the room cozier in winter, and provide a fine place to settle down for storytelling or reading.

13 *Maintain a costume closet.* Old hats, uniforms, costumes, masks, and unusual clothing can be used for class plays, role-playing activities, self-directed dramatizations, and related activities. Such activities are particularly successful when teaching reading. (Yard sales are a great source.)

14 *Start a mail service.* A mailbox somewhere in the classroom enables students to send notes to each other and to the teacher. Also, the teacher can use the mailbox to communicate positive messages to students. (To ensure that some student is not overlooked, the teacher can keep a private roster of student names to check off as notes are sent.)

15 *Assign "can-do" homework.* Students should have a good chance of success with the assigned homework. To assign homework when you believe that students cannot do it is simply causing trouble. The secret is to assign homework that you know students can do. When they ask why, you reply: "Practice, practice, practice is the key to learning."

16 *Build interest in spelling.* A good way to combine social relationships with basic spelling skills is to use the first name of each child in spelling lists. This encourages students to get to know each other while learning how to spell.

17 *Dial-a-parent.* Each week call a parent with some honest and positive report about his or her child. If the parent does not have a telephone, a post-card with the same report will work as well.

18 *Teach something tough.* One of the best ways to invite students to feel good about themselves as learners is to teach them something that others do not know. This is particularly important when working with students labeled slow and placed in special classes. In teaching spelling, for example, the teacher may include a few very difficult words, such as "proselytize" or "proletariat," that even the so-called bright students will not know. Few things are as enhancing as knowledge, particularly when students are trying desperately to avoid the label *slow learner* or *retard*.

19 *Use the newspaper.* Watch the newspaper for articles dealing with students and families, their interests, and the course content. Clipping newspaper articles and sharing them with students—even sending a holiday or other special greeting to the class by placing a classified ad in the local paper—can be effective both as a means of expressing positive feelings and as a way of encouraging students to read.

20 *Share collections*. Almost every student has collected something—cans, rocks, dolls, matchbox covers. Collecting can lead to all sorts of marvelous learning and future careers. Encourage students to begin collections. If a student already has a collection, invite him or her to display it in the school.

21 *Make an I Can*. Cover a small fruit-juice can with bright contact paper. Paste a picture of an eye cut from a magazine on the outside of the can. When a student says "I can't," give the student an I Can. The I Can is good to keep pencils in and to remind the student that "I can!"

22 *Avoid the /wh/ bird*. When working with young children, avoid an overabundance of who, what, or why questions. The young child is likely to interpret such questions as an accusation that he or she has done something wrong.

23 *Eat the alphabet*. Kindergarten and first-grade children can have fun finding a food that begins with a certain letter. Start with "A" (apple? angel-food cake?) and try to work through the alphabet, one letter at a time. Of course, the students help in finding the right letters!

24 *Spread positive rumors*. Note something positive a student does, then describe it to the class without mentioning the student's name. The purpose of positive rumors is to let students know how good they are and how much they can learn. When a teacher remarks, "I noticed how courteous a certain student was this morning," the entire class is complimented.

25 *Wish happy summer birthdays*. Sometimes people in schools who have summer birthdays get neglected. To avoid this, on the last day of school have all summer birthday people stand while everyone sings "Happy Birthday" to them.

What Food-Service Professionals Can Do

1 *Use bright, warm colors to invite.* This is true in even the most meager surroundings. Bright color is a real pick-up for the school cafeteria. Invite the students and faculty for a painting party on a Saturday morning. You supply the brunch.

2 *Offer comfortable seating.* Your seating arrangement can have a definite effect on atmosphere. Make sure there is adequate space between tables. Eighteen inches between chair backs is recommended when diners are seated.

3 *Have music.* Soft, appropriate music can make the time spent in your cafeteria more relaxing. It could even brighten your steps!

4 *Hang live plants.* Attractive hanging baskets and other plants make any cafeteria come alive. They can help develop a homey atmosphere in your cafeteria. Students can help with their care.

5 *Remember your basics of menu planning.* Consider the food characteristics of color, texture, consistency, flavor combination, shape, and method of preparation. Do the combinations from your menu make an attractive and pleasing wholesome meal?

6 *Consider the appearance of your food.* Appearance alone can be changed by the garnishes and condiments used with food. Try some thing different, such as fresh fruit and vegetables. Be imaginative!

7 *Remember that variety is the spice of life.* Offering the same foods over and over is one of the most common faults in menu planning. Experiment, use foods that are in season, and take a chance! You and your guests may be pleasantly surprised.

8 *Provide caloric information.* What are the calories of the entrees and other items being served? This information will be particularly useful to weight-conscious persons.

9 *Offer specific combinations of low-calorie plates.* You could even provide a few nutrition-education tidbits to go along with them.

10 *Celebrate birthdays.* Prepare a big sheet cake once a month for students whose birthdays fall in that month. If you have the energy, you could have a cupcake for each birthday student.

11 *Work with the community.* Get involved with special community activities. Make a special day to honor older adults by having students invite their grandparents or an older adult to visit the school and have lunch.

12 *Seek out assistance.* Discover new information from your colleagues. Visit other school cafeterias. Join professional organizations. Keep abreast of the latest technology and ideas in both nutrition and food service.

13 *Have taste tests.* Students can help judge on a regular basis. This will allow students and food service staff to get better acquainted, will encourage the students to see how the kitchen operates, and most important, will function as a source of student input.

14 *Work through student groups.* These are usually the leaders of the school and can certainly help to make the cafeteria more inviting. You might even organize a student food-service professional club.

15 *Smile!* A friendly smile from each food-service professional can add to the flavor of any meal.

16 *Keep fresh bulletin boards.* Attractive bulletin boards in the cafeteria that are bright, up-to-date, and informative can add to learning and to the beauty of the area.

17 *Remember the holidays.* Holidays are sprinkled throughout the school year. They offer special ways to invite creatively. Christmas, Hanukkah, Ramadan, and Thanksgiving are only a few of the many special events that can be celebrated with special foods, decorations, and themes.

18 *Make the kitchen a learning center.* Many classes can benefit from visiting the kitchen and learning about food preparation procedures. This is also a good way to teach sanitation. In high school, a visit can be used to provide special training for students interested in food service. Students can function as cashiers, typists, cooks, clerks, and servers.

19 *Give some choices.* It seems wasteful to give each person the same amount of the same food. Find ways to allow students to have choices. With planning, it can be done!

20 *Toot your horn.* The cafeteria menus can be placed in newspapers, announcements, bulletin boards, or even announced with the morning PA news.

21 *Remember National School Lunch Week.* This is a good time to host parents. A special program can promote the school lunch program and give parents an opportunity to have lunch with their children.

22 *Fly the school colors.* Where reasonable, use the school colors in bulletin boards, painted walls, and even, on special occasions, the food!

23 *Greet your guests.* Have at least one person to speak a friendly greeting to each student as he or she moves down the cafeteria line. And do not forget a thank-you at the cash register end.

24 *Celebrate other cultures.* African, Chinese, Mexican, Hawaiian, West Indian, Italian, and German cultures are only some of the many whose foods you can salute with your menu. With a little planning, your menu can reflect the academic curriculum.

25 *Wear special uniforms.* We are all familiar with the standard white outfit worn by most food-service professionals. But why not pastels once in awhile? The uniform of the day can be accented for special times such as Halloween, Thanksgiving, and Valentine's Day. Also, an attractive apron can do wonders for the most sterile-looking white uniform.

What Library Media Specialists Can Do

1 *Get involved with curriculum.* Consider your instructional role in the school. Take time to consult with faculty members, participate in interdisciplinary teaming, and let everyone know that you can provide specific books and materials that relate to the curriculum.

2 *Encourage responsible independence.* The library media center represents a place where students can visit alone, check out materials, and be responsible for things in their care. To encourage independence, students should be trusted to move about the school. The other half of independence is responsibility. Students are expected to pay for lost materials.

3 *Teach cooperation.* What better place to teach cooperative activities than the school library media center. The center can provide flexible scheduling that encourages healthy interaction among students. Games, computer activities, and related programs can develop special team skills. Getting cooperating groups from several classes to work together offers exciting possibilities.

4 *Check the job description.* Sometimes library media specialists can find themselves heavily involved in processes or activities that are not related to their professional roles. Help the principal and teachers understand the proper use of the school library and seek their support in using the facilities.

5 *Share success stories.* The typical school library media center is filled with inspiring accounts of successes in spite of great odds. A celebration of success is vital. Encourage students to read books dealing with moral and ethical concerns, and be sure to offer books written by other students.

6 *Provide book marks.* Make available strips of stiff paper so that students can make book marks for themselves and others with decorations, happy holidays, or special quotes on them. Bookmarks can also contain brief book reviews. Bookmarks help prevent folding pages to mark places.

7 *Organize a character day.* Ask students to select a favorite book character and dress as that character for a day. Hold a schoolwide parade of all the characters and video tape the parade for later showing to students, teachers, and parents. (Of course, teachers and staff are also asked to select a character and dress the part.)

8 *Solve the mystery.* Take pictures of characters in books and have them duplicated on paper for four-inch badges. Each library media specialist wears a book character. When a student can identify the character and give accurate information about the character, the student wins the badge. Students will spend hours in the library tracking down unfamiliar characters.

9 *Create a user-friendly library.* Often the library media center is located in a highly visible area of the school. Be sure to provide lots of attractive displays, warm colors, student art shows, and comfortable furniture for students of all ages.

10 *Send acceptance signals.* Like classroom teachers, library media specialists can work to know students by name and ask as many as possible to serve as student helpers and assistants.

11 *Flex the time schedule.* Providing flexible times for students to visit the library adds greatly to the average daily circulation of books. This means flexing the class and bus schedules. There are early and late busses for athletic teams, why not the library? Be creative with time by opening the library before, during, and after school, including lunchtime.

12 *Give books away.* It is advantageous for the library specialist to have some paperback books to give away as gifts or special recognition of students. This requires a good collection of books at a variety of reading levels. Give books away as you learn what students like.

13 *Maintain a "Brag Book."* Keep an album in the library media center of all current newspaper articles involving students, teachers, staff, and alumni. The Brag Book should include all activities and honors that take place during the school year. At the end of the academic year, the Brag Book can be placed in the school media center archives.

14 *Encourage bibliotherapy.* Arrange a special area in the school library for books that address current teen problems. Be sure to include book sections on health issues, interpersonal relations, conflict management, and what its like to be the "new kid on the block" or "living with a kid sister or brother."

15 *Organize a poetry break.* In elementary schools, work with the teachers to arrive in class unannounced and read several poems. The right poem at the right moment can leave a lifelong impression.

16 *Become a story teller.* Few things are as popular in the elementary grades as having a story read to students. This is particularly true when the media specialist "hams" it up with dramatic gestures and dress.

17 *Ask students to evaluate materials.* Ask students to review reading materials being considered for the library, and pay careful attention to their reviews. What is appealing to adults might not be appealing to students. Asking for evaluations and recommendations regarding reading material is likely to call forth a feeling of importance in students.

18 *Pass it on.* Every time anyone uses anything in the media center, encourage them to complete a brief evaluation of its usefulness and attractiveness. Arrange a system where a review form is included with each book checked out. This review form offers comments for the next person who checks this book out.

19 *Form linkages.* Work cooperatively with other resource people both within and outside the local school system. Technology is changing so rapidly that the library media specialist must work even harder just to keep up with the information highway.

20 *Picture the staff.* To help students and teachers know the library workers, design a bulletin board with caricatures of each staff member engaged in an out-of-school special interest. This enables students to identify potential interests and people who can provide assistance.

21 *Search out lost souls.* Often students (and teachers) are confused and overwhelmed when they come to the library. Rather than waiting for them to come to you, be proactive and walk around to see if you can help.

22 *Give it that touch of home.* Libraries can become very "institutional." One way to make the library more like a place for an inviting family is to deinstitutionalize it. This may include getting some comfortable stuffed chairs and some table lamp lighting—both of which can be gotten at garage sales, along with lots of other "homey" stuff.

23 *Keep it simple—and colorful.* The audiovisual equipment runs best if people know how to use it. Demonstrate a different piece of equipment at each faculty meeting. Have a different colored set of instructions available for each piece of library equipment for those who may need a reminder. Color-code the equipment to match the instructions.

24 *Form a book-of-the-month club.* Schools have a variety of clubs, so why not have one for people who like to read and talk about their books? Invite teachers, staff, and community members to join this club and show some of their books. You can come up with a top-ten list of books checked out each month.

25 *Make it a personal closing.* Rather than flicking the lights or using a bell, walk around the library and let people know it is closing time as they do in English Pubs: Announce, "Time, ladies and gentlemen." You may establish a tradition.

What Middle School Teachers Can Do

1 *Prime the pump.* Initial contacts with students are very important. Call, if possible, or write each student even before school starts. Introduce yourself and welcome the student to our school. Invitations can start early.

2 *Share decisions.* Where possible, involve others in the decision-making process. Students can participate in such areas as conduct rules, academic expectations, activities, even textbook reviews and teacher selection. The main point is to make it our school, where we have some influence on what happens to us.

3 *Solve the mystery.* A good ice-breaker is to invite the class members to write something about themselves that is unusual. These clues should be written in sentence form and the folded clues placed in a box. Pass the clues around, each person receiving one clue. Now let all "detectives" try to locate their person.

4 *Start a trading library.* Set up a small library in your classroom where students can donate books and take turns serving as librarian. Explain to students that books are meant to be used and enjoyed. The library promotes both sharing and reading.

5 *Form some triads.* Divide your class into groups of threes called triads. Ask each triad to research, obtain materials, and teach a mini-lesson on the selected course subject. Triads invite new friendships, break down barriers, and encourage learning.

6 *Communicate positively.* Too often the majority of messages sent to parents are essentially negative: "Bill forgot his gym socks," "Lucy was late again." To avoid emphasizing the negative, make a vow that most personal notes going home will be positive: "Bill is making great progress in rope-climbing," "Lucy has written some beautiful little poems." In a child's life there are no little successes or failures—everything counts.

7 *Keep on schedule.* A small clock somewhere in your classroom will help to budget your time and energies. In an office, it is best to place the clock behind the chair the guest will use so you can be aware of time schedules without consulting your wristwatch—which can be a very disinviting act.

8 *Lower the volume.* If you raise your voice when the discipline begins to break down, then practice lowering your voice when you want attention. The surprise works almost every time.

9 *Demonstrate your fallibility.* Be willing to express your own lack of knowledge on a particular subject and to ask students for help in arriving at understandings. By modeling that "no one is perfect," you invite students to risk trying and making mistakes in order to develop.

10 *Cool down first.* Teachers who practice invitational education avoid responding to a situation while angry or upset. It is important to let tempers cool down a little before answering, particularly when you're putting something in writing.

11 *Relate to people, not labels.* Be cautious in substituting the label for the person. For example, a person might be exhibiting very disinviting behavior, but this does not mean that the person is a disinviting person. Sometimes labels can be worse than the problem itself.

12 *Post college offerings.* Keep up to date on classes taught at neighboring colleges and universities, particularly in your professional field. By posting these offerings, you invite your fellow professionals to take advantage of them as well. Better still, organize a carpool for attending them.

13 *Hold a fractions party.* Bring (or ask the class to bring) some pies, square cakes, or other goodies and invite students to recognize the differences among $3/4$, $5/8$, $1/2$, or $1/3$. (They get to eat their answers.) It will not take long for every student to learn there is quite a difference between $2/3$ and $1/3$!

14 *Sock it to 'em.* Ask each student to bring an old sock to school. Place the sock over a shoe and wear it for a walk. Next, wet all the socks and place them in the sun. Something will soon grow! This little exercise invites student interest in the natural sciences.

15 *Build a poem.* Writing a sixteen-line poem can seem like an impossible task to some students. To avoid the problem, ask each student to write a one-line poem on an agreed-upon topic (a sunset is an excellent subject). Collect the one-line poems and select a small group of students to put the lines into a poem. The result is usually outstanding.

16 *Place a mirror on the wall.* Obtain a full-length mirror and place it somewhere in the classroom where students can see themselves as they pass by. This promotes neatness and a sense of grooming among young people.

17 *Visit a graveyard.* To encourage writing and imagination, take a field trip to an old graveyard. Ask the students to study the stones, then select one to write about. "What was the person like? What happened in his or her life? How was life at that time?" Higher-grade students can conduct actual research in library files, old newspapers, and the like.

18 *Take a sound walk.* Invite your students to take a sound walk with you. Have each student take a piece of paper and sit in a quiet place. Ask the students to list all the sounds they can hear that occur in nature. Also, list on the same paper all the sounds made by humans. Later, they can pair off and compare their answers, and then pairs can join other pairs to share.

19 *Invite writing.* Ask students to write stories about themselves. Collect the stories along with poems and drawings and bind them with laminated cardboard. The completed books can be taken home as gifts, or placed in the school library for others to check out. The process encourages writing and a special feeling of importance.

20 *Buy greetings at half price.* Christmas, Hanukkah, Valentine's Day, and other holiday cards always go on sale immediately after the holiday is over. This is a very good time to buy cards for next year's mailing to students, colleagues, and friends.

21 *Discover a salad bar.* Check around and locate a restaurant that provides a luncheon salad bar. If you and your colleagues are able to leave campus during lunch, form a luncheon party. An inexpensive and refreshing salad luncheon is good for you and provides a pleasant time for mutual support and professional development.

22 *Begin a museum.* Start a special file of letters, awards, or treasures that you have received during your teaching career. When you begin to feel a little blue or begin to doubt your own worth, visit your museum. It will lift your spirits, renew your faith in your own ability, and help you to help others.

23 *Handle the unacceptable.* When a student has submitted something unacceptable, try this approach: "I think you can do better than this." Point out ways the work can be improved, then say: "Will you try again?" This encourages both student responsibility and academic success.

24 *Swap a teacher.* Arrange to trade positions with a teacher from another school for a week. This will enrich everyone—the school, the teacher who volunteers to participate, and the students involved. It is a good way to avoid the early spring "blahs."

25 *Maintain a model classroom.* Classrooms are usually stripped of all decorations during the summer to allow workers to clean and paint. Summer is often the time when new students and parents visit the school, so suggest that the classroom closest to the office be beautifully decorated during summer. The principal can take incoming students and parents to this room to show them how inviting the whole school will look come fall.

What Physical Educators Can Do

1 *Share a lap.* When most of us were growing up, being ordered by the coach to "take a lap" in gym class was a form of punishment. It can be made into a treat when the student is invited by the coach to "take a lap with me." Jogging around the track with the coach can build a fine sense of fellowship.

2 *Play that funky music.* Use music to add tempo to warm-up exercises. Let students bring their favorite records in to provide the beat to which they move as they exercise. This adds a new and exciting dimension to exercising and can help make an otherwise boring activity somewhat more enjoyable.

3 *Share stuff.* In the classroom health part of physical education (grades seven through nine), maintain a collection of health magazines, books, and articles as well as sports literature that may interest the age group for check-out or free-time reading.

4 *Have a manager for each week.* Encourage group and individual responsibility and cooperation by inviting a group of students (or an individual student) to be your assistants for a week. Encourage your assistants to share in planning the week's activities as well as supervising equipment.

5 *Keep students up.* Keep students abreast of what is happening in the news in health, sports, and physical activities. Information about sports tournaments, such as the World Series, the Super Bowl, or national events, may promote interest and prompt reading. On special occasions, such as the Olympics, present a mini-unit on the event's history and the training involved.

6 *Keep the gym fresh.* Solicit the custodians' special help in having pride in helping to keep the gym, locker rooms, and shower areas as clean and fresh-smelling as possible. Doing your part in cleaning may invite extra effort by the custodian. Also, the words *please* and *thank you* will encourage the special help you need in keeping the gym clean.

7 *Be audiovisual-minded.* Use physical education activity films as a change of pace in teaching. Let students see the various steps in accomplishing a specific skill. If available, use a videotape machine. This tool provides excellent feedback and allows each student to see the benefits of working together as well as measuring individual progress.

8 *Bring the history of sports to life.* Ask students to draw posters depicting historical aspects or highlights of the particular sport in season. This is also applicable to special or unusual events in sports. You can use this effectively to introduce a new sports activity that is being taught or to point out little-known facets of a traditional sport.

9 *Show the world of sports.* To add excitement and invite learning, secure special film highlights (usually free of charge) of sporting events such as the Men's and Women's National Basketball Championships. Your students are likely to be inspired to new achievements by watching these exciting events.

10 *Lend a helping hand.* If physical education uniforms are required, try to provide (in a discreet manner) clean used or new uniforms for those who cannot afford them. In most schools, the administration will easily approve this.

11 *Invite new students.* When a new student enrolls in class, take a few minutes before class to find out a few pertinent and positive things, such as what town the student has come from, personal interests, whether the student is an athlete or club member, and where the student resides now. Then introduce the student to the class and share positive tidbits of information.

12 *Go on activity trips.* Arrange outside trips in conjunction with a teaching unit. For example, provide the opportunity for games at a bowling alley, roller rink, ice-skating arena, putt-putt golf, or even a tour of a regulation golf course. You can also relatively easily arrange group attendance at nearby college varsity sports activities.

13 *Look for the causes of problems.* It is important to work on causes of problems in schools. These causes are not always student misbehavior. For example, being late to class from a shower in physical education may be caused by late dismissal from gym or not enough time allowed for class changing. Changing the system or reevaluating your actions can sometimes eliminate problems.

14 *Try an alphabet soup exercise.* One way to avoid boredom when directing calisthenics is to divide students into groups of three. Next, call out a letter in the alphabet and ask each triad to make that letter using their bodies.

15 *Improve the office.* Provide an attractive, uncluttered office (as best you can) with signs inviting students to come in. In the best interests of teaching and privacy, it may help to indicate specific times (office hours) when you are more available for chatting and personal discussions.

16 *Keep the vision.* See students as they can be, not as they are. Too often physical educators say: "Do your best" when "You can do better, so practice" can be a more powerful invitation to realize potential. Every student is in the process of becoming, so it is important for physical educators to invite them to become in positive directions.

17 *Vary your grading system.* Grading systems can be modified to place major emphasis on effort, attitude, cooperation, and fair play. You might discover that if you have the students work on these aspects of their development, the skill and performance aspects of physical education will fall into place.

18 *Be a social director.* Periodically provide opportunities for teachers to participate right along with students. These may include such social activities as basketball free-throw shooting contests, Ping-Pong, or golf. These activities provide the means by which teacher-teacher and teacher-student social interactions are encouraged.

19 *Watch for help signs.* Watch for "I-need-help" signs among the students. If you notice a student who wants to learn a skill, but is having difficulty doing so, discreetly offer to help after class or after school.

20 *Invite variety.* Vary the standard rules of traditional games in creative ways. This takes some rigidity out of the expected and increases participation, success, and excitement.

21 *Be a showcase for talent.* Provide opportunities for a school-wide display of acquired skills or talents such as tumbling, gymnastics, or modern dance. Strive for group recognition and effort as well as individual spotlighting. These opportunities for displaying students' talents come at school assemblies, PTA programs, and community club meetings.

22 *Advertise your students' activities.* Use the school newspaper to communicate special activities, awards, and events taking place in your physical education class. These may include the names of assistants, the student of the week or month, skills records, feats, and accomplishments. Make announcements of special sporting events coming up within the school or community as well as the schedule of upcoming physical education activities.

23 *Post class achievements and honors.* Assign one gym bulletin board the special title of "Physical Education Bulletin Board." Note any skills records, accomplishments, and feats of students in your class. Names and pictures of physical education assistants and specially recognized students may be displayed here also. It may even be fun to take a class photograph early in the year and post it. Then you have it to look back on as the year progresses.

24 *Invite special interests.* Help form and sponsor special interest groups such as a jogging club (in the morning before school, at lunchtime, or after school), a bike-riding club for those who cycle to school (after school and weekends), or a sports event club to decorate bulletin boards for the sports in season. This group might also be responsible for posting a calendar of coming school and local sports events such as foot races, bike races, gymnastics club tryouts, or a school Ping-Pong tournament and related activities.

25 *Work for gender equality.* Ensure that girls are given as much encouragement and as many opportunities as boys to develop physically. These encouragements and opportunities should take the form of equal sports facilities, financial support, number and nature of activities, and equal number of coaches, with equal pay.

What School Administrators Can Do

1 *Organize a back-to-school party.* Plan a faculty and staff party to take place before school begins. This coming together can be a simple covered-dish, BYOB sort of get-together to renew friendships, introduce new colleagues, and set the stage for a successful academic year.

2 *Celebrate each day.* When each new school day begins, the school administrator can walk around the school, salute the buses as they arrive, check the grounds, and make a special point of stopping at every classroom to say "Good morning" to students and teachers. (If the administrator is really energetic, he or she can say "So long, see you tomorrow" to students as they depart for home each day.) This habit invites a good feeling in students and faculty.

3 *Jack up the faculty meeting.* Everyone can make a vow that all faculty meetings will start on time and will never go over one hour. One simple technique to enforce the rule is for everyone to stand at the fifty-five minute mark and continue standing until the end of the meeting. It will not go over an hour!

4 *Improve the teachers' lounge.* Teachers benefit from having a comfortable place to relax. Do what you can to make the lounge more inviting. A living plant, a bowl of flowers, an area rug, fresh paint, clean windows, a baked cake are among the many things that can make the "recovery room" more like a real place to relax.

5 *Float the faculty meeting.* Move the faculty meeting around the school and meet in different environments. This gives a freshness to meetings and a new outlook on problems. It also helps to get everyone involved. And no matter where you meet, remember to arrange for something to eat and drink. The "care and feeding" of faculty is most important. Even such simple fare as coffee, juice, cookies, and fruit can contribute to a successful meeting.

6 *Share successes.* Begin each faculty meeting with a report of all the honest success experiences that have taken place since the last meeting.

Ask teachers and other professionals to share their success experiences. This process helps to start each meeting off on a positive note.

7 *Visit the provinces.* The school administrator is responsible for the entire school, not just the principal's office. Visit the teacher's lounge, gym, cafeteria, furnace room, shops, labs, classrooms, and grounds frequently. Discipline is best handled before it becomes a problem, and the secret is to be visible. Besides, you don't need an invitation to visit your school!

8 *Be a booster.* The school administrator's time is severely limited, but his or her presence at a play, band concert, athletic contest, or other student activity can be seen as a most inviting act. When students (and parents) perceive the school administrator as interested in their activities, they will probably feel more invited by the school.

9 *Invite action, not inaction.* Too often principals, like teachers, give directions that could best be followed by pet rocks: "Don't leave your class unattended," "Stop smoking in the faculty dining area," "Quit questioning school policies." With such directions, a pet rock would make the ideal teacher. Asking faculty and staff to do something is much better than telling them what not to do.

10 *Take a dare.* When the school plans a program involving faculty— faculty-student basketball game, skit program, fun night, raffle day—why not accept a part? Even though you can't do everything, you can always do something to make the family spirit come alive in your school.

11 *Send unconditional invitations.* Often we are guilty of sending invitations to students that suggest we really doubt acceptance. For example, "You can join the club if you want to," "You are welcome, but we are leaving early," "I think you can learn this; however, you'll have to pay the price" all suggest conditional regard. It is usually better to send unconditional invitations, simple declarative statements of support: "I know you can do this."

12 *Be explicit with your invitations.* The more explicit a request, the more it lends itself to acceptance. Sometimes principals create misunderstandings by being vague. Others wonder "What was meant by that?" When the principal is explicit with his or her invitations, the likelihood of success increases. For example, the principal who says, "John, I want you to do this, will you do it?" has a good chance of having his or her invitation accepted.

13 *Invite cooperation with other schools.* If you wish to bring in a well-known speaker or consultant, one way to reduce the expense and responsibility involved is to ask neighboring school systems or related organizations to share in sponsoring the visit. This makes good money sense, encourages cooperation, increases attendance, and may result in your being invited by your educational neighbors later.

14 *Use the yearbook.* School yearbooks are a great source of names and faces. By spending some time looking through the yearbook and relating names to faces, you'll be in a better position to learn the names of many of your students in a relatively short time and to practice using those names at every opportunity.

15 *Celebrate life.* Birthdays of students, teachers, and staff can be marked on a private calendar in readiness for a special greeting. (Even the grouchiest teacher will light up when he or she is given a surprise party.) And don't forget to celebrate the appearance of a new baby or other special event in the lives of students, staff, or faculty.

16 *Feed the feeders.* Send copies of honor rolls, student work, awards, outstanding papers, and related material to teachers in the feeder schools. This lets them know that you are aware of their major contributions to the success of your school.

17 *Keep a mug file.* Start a card file on members of the school's professional family, including teachers, aides, custodians, cafeteria staff, bus drivers, counselors—every adult who serves the school system. A single index card can hold a wealth of information about the people with whom the school administrator comes in contact. On each card list personal items, such as name of spouse, number of children, hobbies, interests. From time to time go through the file, add information, check that you have visited with everyone recently. If you have missed anyone, make a special effort to go and chat with that person. In a large school, it is helpful to make a notation each time you visit with a person.

18 *Reduce line time.* Develop a plan that will permit faculty, staff, and students to avoid long lines in the cafeteria. Time in school is too valuable to spend in line. In fact, the time spent on learning tasks is one of the most important ingredients in children's success in school. A flexible lunch period schedule gives people a choice of what time they want to go to lunch. Parents can help with flexible lunch arrangements.

19 *Place some welcome decals.* The Midwest Specialties Company (P.O. Box 2026, Kalamazoo, Michigan 49001) sells decals for glass and solid doors. The decals read "Welcome to our school—Visitors please report to the main office upon entering the building during regular school hours. Thank you." This sign is certainly more professionally inviting than "Visitors Must Report to Office" or "No Trespassing."

20 *Recognize support personnel.* Crossing guards, bus drivers, cafeteria workers, custodians, and other noninstructional staff are vital to the school; let them know how important they are by inviting them to meetings, or have a luncheon or other special recognition for them. They all contribute significantly to the inviting or disinviting environment of the school.

21 *Organize a Saturday planting party.* Ask everyone in the school to come to school on a Saturday morning to help improve the school's appearance with plants and flowers. Parents, students, and others can bring bedding plants. Even nurseries may donate a plant or two. School service clubs and garden clubs can also be invited to participate and join the party.

22 *Hold those calls.* When the school executive is with a visitor, it is a most inviting act for the executive to say to his or her secretary: "Will you please hold incoming calls for the next ten minutes?" This is an indirect way of saying to the visitor: "You are important, and for the next ten minutes, I do not want us to be interrupted."

23 *Say no slowly.* When you must give a negative response to a request, at least let it come after you have listened carefully and fully to the request. One of the worst indictments that can be leveled against an administrator is for someone to say: "The principal wouldn't even listen to me!" The failure even to consider a request, to hear the person out, can hurt more than the negative answer. Invite each person to express his or her request fully before it is accepted or rejected.

24 *Offer refreshments to visitors.* Breaking bread together is an ancient sign of peace and friendship. By offering each visitor to your office some coffee, tea, juice, or light refreshment, the stage is set for resolving problems and facilitating good feelings.

25 *Improve teacher evaluations.* When the principal is planning to observe and evaluate a teacher, it is important to meet with the teacher first and find out what the teacher plans to do. Looking at behavior only, and not at intentions as well, leaves out half the picture.

What School Bus Drivers Can Do

1 *Demonstrate leadership.* Show the students on your bus by your behavior that you care about them, and explain why you need to set guidelines and limits on their activities. Avoid "Because I said so!" It is important that you express to your student riders the belief that they have as much value and responsibility as you do. Every person on the bus, including the driver, has equal value and deserves equal respect. Because it is our bus, we all have responsibility for making it a good place to be.

2 *Develop bus spirit.* At the beginning of the school year invite your riders to decide upon a nickname for the bus. By using the same techniques as an athletic team, a group of riders and the driver can develop a real team spirit.

3 *Be a greeter.* With each school day make it a point to say "Good morning" to each student as he or she steps on the bus. Each afternoon say "So long, see you tomorrow" as each student departs for home. This habit invites a good feeling in every one, including the driver.

4 *Start a chain reaction.* The first student on the bus in the morning greets the next student who arrives; this continues until everyone is on the bus. This helps students to learn the names of their busmates and encourages a friendly environment on the bus.

5 *Use collective, inclusive words.* Using such pronouns as *we*, *us*, and *our* on the bus is much more inviting than using *you*, *yours*, or *mine*. Make it our bus—keeping it clean is up to us. Using the collective term invites a feeling of shared effort.

6 *Point out what's working.* Instead of always pointing out what is wrong, change your focus and point out things that are right. Bus riders learn much more from things that work than they do from things that do not.

7 *Be sensitive with praise.* Not all students are willing or able to accept praise, particularly praise given to them in front of their friends. A private comment to let a student know how pleased you are with his or her behavior might be more appropriate.

8 *Show you care.* When someone is ill or misses the bus for other reasons, a special comment to that student when he or she returns can be a most caring and thoughtful act.

9 *Keep up to date.* Try to keep abreast of fads, fashions, heroes, films, sports, singers, and other current interests of students. This is a good way to show students the driver is "with it."

10 *Check the newspaper.* Watch the newspaper for articles dealing with your riders and their families. Clipping an article and sharing it with a student can be an effective way of expressing your interest.

11 *Personalize some pencils.* For a few dollars you can order pencils with some special greeting, such as "Season's Greetings to you from Mr. Smith." The pencils can be given to your riders the last day before a holiday season. The same idea can be used just before school ends for the summer: "Mrs. Reynolds wishes you a great summer vacation."

12 *Double your pleasure.* As nice as it is to receive kind words directly, it can be even nicer to learn that kind words were spoken about you to someone else. Rather than praise someone directly, praising the person to someone else can have double the impact.

13 *Divide the routes.* Although it is not always possible, buses could be made more inviting if they were smaller and had shorter routes. Having different size buses and routes can benefit everyone and can give added flexibility to the school system.

14 *Keep the bus clean*. Whether they admit it or not, most people enjoy riding in a clean bus. Do what you can to keep the bus clean, and encourage your riders to help. A little trash can or two on the bus (if not forbidden by regulations) can teach students good behavior.

15 *Practice preventive maintenance*. Don't wait until the bus breaks down to take care of problems. Keep the bus in good running order by insisting on good service and safety checks.

16 *Make repairs rather than patch-ups*. Torn seats with tape over them often lead to more torn seats. A professional patching kit works much better than tape. Catching damage early and repairing it well prevents the spread of further damage.

17 *Check the system*. Sometimes the causes of problems in and around buses are not people. Sometimes it is the system. Scheduling buses to leave school within a very few minutes after school ends each day forces students to run, shove, and push to make the bus.

18 *Look sharp and tag up*. Driving a school bus is a professional responsibility and drivers should look the part. A metal name tag for each school bus driver together with a neat and well-groomed appearance identify drivers as professionals.

19 *Keep rules short and simple*. Such simple rules as "Please Remain in Seats," "Please Respect Property," and "Please Speak Softly" can do wonders to maintain the driver's sanity. And remember, the fewer the rules the less likely they are to be broken.

20 *Prepare a birthday box*. For the busy bus driver, a birthday box can be prepared during the summer months. The box contains small, inexpensive, wrapped gifts, nicely decorated. The birthday bus rider chooses a wrapped gift from the box for his or her own on that special day. On the last day of school, students with summer birthdays get to choose a wrapped gift.

21 *Make your bus inviting*. If not against rules, a little bulletin board, a smiley face, an animal cutout, design, or the like can invite the student to feel: "This is our bus. The driver takes pride in it, and so will I."

22 *Help arrange driving programs.* In addition to the usual driver education programs such as safety, maintenance, and the like, ask that training programs for bus drivers include such subjects as driver self-concept, interpersonal relationships, and stress management. This will work to everyone's benefit.

23 *Set an example in politeness.* "Please" and "Thank you" are magic words. When the driver shows respect for the riders, it is likely that riders will begin to respect the driver. Civility and courtesy are critical in operating a bus.

24 *Stress cooperation.* Above everything else, driving a bus is a cooperative act. Without cooperation from other drivers, riders, and the public, driving a bus would be almost impossible. Encourage cooperation by being cooperative.

25 *Be safe.* The number one priority of a school bus driver is to safely transport children to and from school. More important than any of the above suggestions, the driver must be constantly alert to the safety of the riders. It is a special responsibility and honor to care for so many young lives. Practice safety in everything you do.

What School Counselors Can Do

1 *Brighten up the center.* Just because they stuck you in a closet is no reason it has to look like a closet! Hang posters, get some living green plants, make your office a place where people want to come. If you desire to be a professionally inviting counselor, have your counseling center reflect that desire. Have comfortable furniture for both students and adults and no thrones facing undersized chairs!

2 *Protect the single-parent child.* Sometimes schools can discriminate against single-parent children. To guard against this, encourage faculty to ask their students, when engaged in gift-making during Mother's Day or Father's Day activities, to "make a card or gift for someone who is very important in your life." This gives a sense of belonging and purpose to the child who only has one parent, if that.

3 *Hold a professional sharing session.* Plan and conduct a "drop-by" session during which teachers can enjoy refreshments and be involved in a brief training program on such topics as stress reduction, contract grading systems, or other innovative offerings. It need not take long for some quality sharing.

4 *Honor older adults.* One way to honor senior citizens is to have a special day for grandparents and older adults. Students can send special invitations to their grandparents or older adult friends to visit the school, join in classes, and enjoy lunch. The day can end with a special assembly or class program.

5 *Arrange some luncheon dates.* Counselors can arrange to have lunch with a different person or group of persons each day. This can be alternated with administrators, teachers, and students. Breaking bread together and chatting informally can do a lot to improve interpersonal relations in the school.

6 *Check your timing.* Timing is very important in inviting. Too much, too soon, too little, too late can weaken the best invitation. Ask yourself: "What invitation, by whom, is most likely to be accepted by this person at this time?"

7 *Carpool to an adventure.* Is a special lecture, important conference, or other activity taking place in some other area? Perhaps the school can help pay for a meal and gas to send some personnel. When they return from the adventure they might share what they learned with the entire staff.

8 *Hold a faculty breakfast.* In return for a few dollars and a few hours of planning, the entire faculty can meet together for breakfast. If energies permit, perhaps the counselor and a few friends could fix breakfast for everyone. After all, service is what the helping profession is all about.

9 *Send a professional gift.* Need a special gift for a special friend? Subscribe to a professional magazine or journal to be sent to him or her. It is a gift that lasts all year.

10 *Float the bulletin board.* Obtain a large sheet of styrofoam. Place whatever message you select on it using mounted paper letters. Next string several helium balloons to the bulletin board. You now have a floating bulletin board that can travel around the school, popping up at unexpected places.

11 *Give "expert" advice sparingly.* One basic tenet of invitational education is to recognize that every person has the potential of becoming more capable and self-supportive. For this reason, be reluctant in providing ready answers to problems. Counseling and consulting are methods of helping people find alternatives and solutions and of guiding them through decision processes in which they can choose a suitable course of action. Providing answers can be disinviting because such behavior may signal a belief that the person is incapable of making appropriate decisions.

12 *Keep the volcano from erupting.* By being accessible and keeping your eyes and ears open you will have the advantage of sensing when difficulties are approaching. This will enable you to be better prepared to offer help when it is needed. Even more important, it may allow you to use preventive strategies to avoid oncoming problems. The professionally inviting counselor handles little problems before they have a chance to become big ones.

13 *Keep the faith.* It is important that the professional not lose heart in the face of rejection. If an invitation is sent it may or may not be accepted, but if it is not sent then it cannot be accepted. For this and other reasons, be not dismayed, and keep on inviting.

14 *Spread the word.* Write a weekly column for your local newspaper to highlight school activities, special accomplishments, educational ideas, and innovations, and to educate the public generally about the many good things taking place in school.

15 *Invest a penny.* "A penny for your thoughts." Tape a brand-new shiny penny to a small card and send one to each teacher in the school. On the card ask the teachers for their suggestions on how the counseling center and personnel can be of special assistance to them.

16 *Offer extra help.* Many faculty and staff perform tasks that are above and beyond their usual responsibilities. Often these jobs are done because the school cannot afford "extra" services. Lend a hand if you can possibly spare the time. Get down on the floor and paint some posters, hang decorations, chaperone field trips, sweep floors, make some educational games, or do whatever you can to invite a feeling of mutual professional support in your school.

17 *Hold a happy hour.* Open up your center occasionally after school for teachers and others to enjoy refreshments and conversation. If space is limited, go to a larger room. This hour can be an excellent opportunity for the staff to develop a feeling of community as well as a time to present a mini-session of new ideas. These gatherings may be for relaxing, with no business, or they may combine pleasure with some professionally interesting idea.

18 *Include the leadership.* Principals, supervisors, school board members, and others appreciate being invited to the counseling center for activities or events. This builds personal relationships between counselors and other professionals and also allows you to show off the counseling program and guidance activities in your school.

19 *Be accessible.* As a professional person in the school, you provide important services. If you set up office hours that are an imposition to other people, then few people will feel welcome to use counseling services. Also, if you put the "Do Not Disturb" sign on your office door, expect people to become disturbed! Availability is a hallmark of the professionally inviting counselor.

20 *Be visible.* Visibility is an important part of accessibility. You may benefit by being out of your office as much as you are in it. Eat with students in the cafeteria, walk the halls during passing periods, and say hello to the teacher whose room is at the far end of the hall. This may be difficult if you are a secondary school counselor, but it is important to be visible.

21 *Follow up.* If someone comes to you with a problem or shares something of a personal nature, be sure to ask about it later. This can be done formally or informally and takes very little time. The important thing is to express your continued concern and interest.

22 *Strangle the paper monster.* Unfortunately, counselors are sometimes among those who create forms for teachers and students to fill out. Try to keep the methods of communication between you and your fellow professionals and students as easy and simple as possible. Time is precious. It should be valued highly and not spent on relatively unimportant paperwork.

23 *Improve your sign language.* Look at every sign and written communication posted in your counseling center and school. Are they inviting? For example, "Office Closed," "Do Not Disturb," or "Do Not Take Records Out" could be reworded so they convey the message while maintaining warmth and concern. Signs are to give directions; they should be positively worded and courteously stated. Please and Thank You should appear on every directive sign.

24 *Have a yearly review.* At the end of each school year ask all faculty and staff members to note down what they thought went well with the counseling program during the year and where improvements might be made. When this is done in a positive manner, many good ideas can be generated for the coming year.

25 *Hold an open house at the end of the year.* Let friends of education know of your successes by holding an informal open house toward the end of the school year. This provides a special opportunity to inform people about the many good things that were accomplished during the school year.

What School Secretaries Can Do

1 *Keep people posted.* Ensure prompt and accurate communication in your school by using announcements, newsletters, flyers, and bulletin boards to keep everyone informed. Even a small blackboard near the mailboxes can be used to remind people of upcoming events. Use more than one system of communication to reach your audience.

2 *Organize student guides.* School visitors should be met quickly and cordially. Student guides are particularly helpful if the school has many visitors; they can serve as hosts. Escorting parents, substitutes, and other visitors to the places they wish to be and helping them with their needs sets an inviting tone.

3 *Embrace the new teacher.* Although the administration usually acquaints new teachers with policies, experienced secretaries can also meet with new teachers to give them a survival manual of practical suggestions and words of comfort to help make their lives more enjoyable during that first year.

4 *Prepare some tooth fairy envelopes.* If you work in an elementary school, have a special tooth fairy envelope ready for sending home a tooth that comes out at school. A clever little poem signed by the teacher and principal makes a special notice of a tender little moment in a family's life.

5 *Plan comfortable meetings.* A careful check of facilities before an activity begins helps ensure that personal needs are met. These areas include seating, lighting, temperature, materials, restroom facilities, and related items of comfort. People participate best when they feel cared for.

6 *Install a student telephone.* Providing a small convenience for students, such as a centrally located telephone that does not require permission to be used, is a special way to invite students to see themselves as able, valuable, and responsible. The phone can be programmed to take only local calls. Installing a student phone is worth the fairly small cost, as it reflects respect for students. When students are treated with respect, they are more likely to show respect.

7 *Share a phone.* School telephones are sometimes protected as though they were a symbol of power. In many schools, teachers and other professionals do not have access to a private phone, yet they often need one. By making your office phone available to others during appropriate times, you demonstrate an effort to develop a cooperative and caring relationship with your colleagues.

8 *Be prompt and patient.* Promptness and patience in listening are two important qualities of the school secretary. When callers and visitors are listened to patiently and attentively, they are in a much better position to express their needs and concerns, particularly when their presence in the office has been acknowledged promptly and courteously.

9 *Be professionally responsible.* An important way to improve the quality of life in your school is to be ethical in your conduct. Be trustworthy with confidences, follow rules (and if they are bad rules, work to change them), and support your colleagues and the purposes of your school.

10 *Stifle the public address system.* Along with discipline problems, disruptions rank among the biggest frustrations of teachers. Because interruptions can be most disinviting, public address system use should be severely limited. Use of the PA system should be restricted to the first five, or last five, minutes of the learning period. (When the PA is used for announcements, it can also be used for happy messages such as birthdays or the arrival of a new brother or sister.)

11 *Send double-strength compliments.* As nice as it is to receive kind words directly, it is even nicer to learn that kind words about you have been expressed to others. Rather than praising a student directly, praising the student to teachers, parents, or other students (when done sensitively) can be highly effective. The original praise will reach the person with double impact!

12 *Let people know you care.* When someone is ill or misses school for other reasons, a note or postcard can do wonders. Such a message need be nothing more than a sheet of paper containing a cheery note.

13 *Have your name known.* By either wearing a name tag or having a name plaque on your desk, you invite people to speak to a person rather than a position.

14 *Keep the office alive.* A bright and cheerful office offers a pleasant, nonverbal message about the quality of life in a school. Offices can be made more attractive by hanging live plants and having up-to-date reading materials available.

15 *Be a booster.* Attend school events, such as plays, interscholastic and intramural sports, and PTA meetings. Buy some band candy, purchase a yearbook, or donate some time to the school bazaar. Demonstrate your school spirit, and encourage students to do the same!

16 *Signal your handle.* Encourage each person on the school staff and faculty to call you by the same name. It may be disinviting to some teachers if a few call you "Bob" while others address you as "Mr. Jones." Most people want to call you by the name you prefer, so let them know your preference.

17 *Be a craftsperson.* Take pride in every letter or announcement that passes through your hands. Check carefully for spelling, syntax, and grammar. Every communication that goes out from the school represents the school and everyone in it.

18 *Share your attention.* It is important to be accessible to the public, staff, and students. Although some priorities require more of your time, it is essential to let others know when you or someone else will be able to assist them.

19 *Rehearse the future, not the past.* So often when we make a mistake, we go over it again and again in our minds—in effect, practicing the mistake. A better way of handling things is to ask: "How will I handle this problem next time?" By concentrating on future response behavior, we can rehearse the future, not the past.

20 *Follow through promptly.* One of the most significant characteristics of the professionally inviting secretary is that he or she follows through promptly. The most positive action, when long delayed, loses much of its reward value.

21 *Make the telephone your ally.* Most contacts with the school are by telephone and so it is important to be professional, personal, and positive. By answering the phone "Good morning, Jefferson High School, Ms. Bradley speaking" you accomplish all three. Saying "I don't know where the principal is; he hasn't been here all day" could be better stated: "The principal is out of the office at the moment; may I help?" Another example: "You'll have to call back" might be replaced with "The principal is in a meeting. May I have your number so she can call you back as soon as the meeting is over?" Convey the message that the caller is important.

22 *Promote positive public relations*. It's never a matter of whether or not the school has public relations, it's a matter of what kind! To promote positive public relations, make sure that the large majority of messages are stated affirmatively and clearly.

23 *Use the pinking shears*. Pinking shears can be used to cut out some of the more beautiful pictures and messages written on the holiday cards you receive. These pictures and messages can be used to decorate an office for all occasions. They also make great note cards.

24 *Distribute resources efficiently and fairly*. Efficient resource allocation is essential to success. Moreover, it is something over which the secretary has direct control. Be as fair-minded as possible in providing material support to faculty and staff.

25 *Know your stuff*. Finding, organizing, and sharing with proper authorities all the information needed to run a school is an important way in which secretaries are professionally inviting. Careful record-keeping and office organization benefit everyone in the school.

What Secondary-School Teachers Can Do

1 *Express your pleasure*. At the beginning of the term, why not tell your students how pleased and honored you are to share their company during the semester? The students may never have heard this from a teacher before. It will bowl them over, and you are off to a good school year.

2 *Develop class spirit*. Early in the school year the teacher can invite the class to decide upon a name for the group. The class might also select an emblem, motto, and class colors. These can be used on the outside of the classroom door, for classroom displays, and on messages to parents and students. By using many of the same techniques as athletic teams, a class can develop team spirit.

3 *Share names*. A way to reduce threat at the beginning of the year is to encourage students to learn more about each other. To do this the teacher can ask students to tell the others in the group about their name. For example: "For whom were you named?" "What does your name mean?" "Does your name seem to fit you?" "Do you like your name?" "Have you ever been kidded about your name or had it mispronounced?" "What do you like to be called?" This simple ice-breaker invites students to talk about themselves in a nonthreatening manner. Also, students are likely to be interested if they are encouraged to look up the etymology of their names in reference books.

4 *Invite dialogue*. Explain to students that "It's not the answers to my questions that are important, it's the questions you have for my answers." Knowledge is constantly unfolding, and today's accepted fact may soon become tomorrow's outmoded concept. Students grow intellectually by challenging ideas.

5 *Hold contests*. For a few minutes (at the beginning or end of a class session) hold a contest to loosen things up. For example, a contest for the most terrible pun or most trivial trivia can invite a warm and friendly class feeling.

6 *Be with it*. Make an effort to understand the world in which today's student lives. For example, try to keep up with fads, fashions, popular heroes, latest films, sports, TV programs, actors, singers, and other current interests of students. Using an instance from some TV program to invite learning of some academic concept can be quite effective.

7 *Tap expertise*. Your school cafeteria worker may be a classical music bug, the bus driver an amateur artist, the school psychologist or nurse a rock collector, the principal a woodworker, your fellow teacher a ballet dancer. Find the talents of people in school and invite these people into your class to share their interests and lives with students.

8 *Rearrange space*. No matter how attractive, your room decorations and layout get stale. Change things around periodically, and be sure to ask those who share your space to assist in the planning and rearranging.

9 *Use the opaque.* An under-utilized audiovisual aid in most schools is the opaque projector. With this simple machine you can reproduce almost any drawing or photograph in almost any larger size. You can fill an entire wall with a map of Europe or show how a bill goes through Congress. Any drawing—with an opaque projector, large white paper, and students with magic markers who trace the projected drawing—can brighten the learning environment.

10 *Encourage participation.* When some students are not participating, try dividing and subdividing the class. Start out with pairs, then groups of four, later groups of eight and sixteen. It is difficult to remain silent when you are 50 percent of a group!

11 *Maintain a giveaway library.* Books are meant to be used and enjoyed. You can encourage reading by reading an occasional passage or brief section from a favorite book, then presenting the book to a student as a gift. Teachers may keep a fresh stock of books on hand by visiting garage sales, flea markets, and Goodwill Industries shops. It is worth the small cost when a student hears a teacher say, "Here's a book I want you to have and enjoy. I think it was written just for you!"

12 *Collect junk.* While looking for books at flea markets and garage sales, also look for objects that can be taken apart, put back together, manipulated—things like broken typewriters, clocks, and simple mechanical devices. Puzzles, toys, and gadgets can all be used to encourage imagination, develop simulation games, and invite learning. These activities have the potential for encouraging learning while inviting positive changes in self-concept.

13 *Make and take.* An unusual invitation involves the production of something. A California teacher has students invest in the stock market and share results. Another teacher in Florida introduces students to geometry by making pancakes and dividing them in various ways. One student exclaimed after class, "Boy, this was the best math lesson I ever ate."

14 *Share duties.* Students can help the teacher with many small tasks. For example, taking roll, distributing and collecting materials, preparing experiments, even evaluation of work can involve students and make the teacher's life a little easier.

15 *Ask "What would you like to learn to do?"* Ask students this question on a short survey form. Where possible, plan and conduct minicourse electives for once-a-week sessions to meet the indicated interests. Learning Asian cooking, studying photography, or attending a seminar on a special topic can be an excellent entree to English essays or mathematical problem solving. These special interest programs would supplement and support well-designed academic courses and programs.

16 *Arrange a "big pal" program.* Tutoring and related activities seem to help both the tutor and the one being tutored. Therefore, arrange a program in which high-school students are matched with students from lower grades to offer support, assistance, and friendship.

17 *Open-end your questions.* By asking questions that require more than a yes-or-no answer, the teacher invites discussion and dialogue. For example, "What do you think about . . .?" and "How would you describe . . .?" generate thinking and involvement.

18 *Now a word from our sponsor.* Divide the class into small film companies and ask each company to prepare a one-minute commercial on an academic concept. Invite each company to write, direct, and video-tape their commercial for class viewing. This process gives both academic learning and class enthusiasm. It also encourages creativity.

19 *Organize an emergency packet.* When you are faced with a no-good or very disinviting day, have an emergency packet ready that contains a few sure-fire lesson plans and enjoyable materials. It can save your sanity.

20 *Share your person.* Let the students know that you have many dimensions other than just teacher. Share anecdotes about your family or pets. Let students know your feelings about books or movies, even share your moods. You will be surprised at how thoughtful and caring students can be when you tell them you have a headache and "Please be gentle with me."

21 *Involve students in decisions*. If your system is one in which teachers select textbooks, ask students of varying backgrounds and achievement to help preview textbooks before decisions are made. After all, who knows better than students which books are inviting? Students can also participate in the decision-making process in other areas, such as rules of conduct, academic expectations, and even teacher selection!

22 *Use a Zen koan*. Zen masters use koans to invite their students to reflect deeply on one's self and one's relation to the world. A koan is a simple question that has no simple answer. It is the student's struggle with the koan, not the master's teaching, that enlightens the student.

23 *Be the greeter, be the leave-taker*. At the beginning and end of each class session, take a minute or two to establish a caring environment. Share a thought, talk about a current event, ask about things; let students know we are human beings first, and teachers or students second.

24 *Use collective, inclusive pronouns*. Using such pronouns as *we*, *us*, and *our* in class seems to be more inviting than using *you* or *yours*. For example, a teacher says: "We've got to get our work done so we can move along." This seems preferable to: "You students must get your work done." Using the collective term invites a feeling of family.

25 *Change color*. If you use red ink or pencil to grade papers, switch to a felt-tip marker, highlighter, or to any color other than red. The color red has negative connotations to many students.

B

Inviting and Disinviting Signals

The following lists of inviting and disinviting verbal comments personal behaviors, physical environments, and printed signs have been identified by educators and students as indicators of the quality of life in schools. These lists are only illustrative, but the presence or absence of items on these lists may help to identify the inviting or disinviting stance taken by those who live and work in and around schools. These items may also serve as a checklist for those in schools who are already doing good things and who want to do them even better.

Verbal Comments

Forty Inviting Comments

Good morning.
Thanks very much.
Congratulations.
Let's talk it over.
How can I help?
Tell me about it.
I appreciate your help.
Happy birthday!
I enjoy having you here.
I understand.
We missed you.
I'm glad you came by.
I like that idea!
I think you can.
Welcome.
I like what you did.
Welcome back.
You are unique.
That's even better.
I've been thinking about you.
How are things going?
How are you?
I'd like your opinion.
Happy holiday!
What do you think?
Let's have lunch.
What can I do for you?
Of course I have time.
That's OK.
I am impressed!
You made me feel good.
Yes.
Please come in.
I've always got time for you.
I think you can do it.
Please tell me more.
May I help you?
Let's do it together.
Come back soon!
I enjoy our time together.

Forty Disinviting Comments

Keep out.
What Mary is trying to say is . . .
Use your head.
It won't work.
You'll have to call back.
You can't do that.
I don't care what you do.
Not bad for a girl.
Don't be so stupid.
Who do you think you are?
He can't be disturbed.
Why didn't you stay at home?
Woman driver.
They don't want to learn.
They don't have the ability.
You can't be that dumb.
They're all right in their place.
Who's calling?
You should not feel that way.
You ought to know better.
You must do as I say.
How could you?
Shape up or ship out.
Anybody can do that.
Why do you bother coming to school?
That's a childish viewpoint.
That is dead wrong.
Hi Chubby.
You goofed.
Get lost.
That's stupid.
So what?
Because I said so, that's why.
What you again?
Forget it.
You'll never make it.
Sit down and shut up.
Knock it off.
What's your excuse this time?
Cool it!

Personal Behaviors

Forty Inviting Behaviors	*Forty Disinviting Behaviors*
Being relaxed	Giving a thumbs-down sign
Lending a book	Interrupting
Smiling	Looking at your watch
Asking for an opinion	Yawning in someone's face
Listening carefully	Shaking your finger at someone
Shaking hands	Scowling and frowning
Opening a door for someone	Slamming a door
Nodding affirmation	Using ridicule
Sharing lunch together	Turning your back on someone
Being on time	Cutting people short
Sending a thoughtful note	Making fun of a person
Bringing a gift	Looking away from someone
Sharing an experience	Leaving someone to answer the phone
Accepting praise	Hitting someone
Giving wait-time	Being obscene
Offering to help	Laughing at someone's misfortune
Yielding interest	Throwing paper on the ground
Providing specific praise	Tapping a pencil (fidgeting)
Learning names	Chewing gum loudly
Offering refreshments	Breaking a promise
Sending a valentine	Forgetting an important date
Providing gentle reminders (where appropriate)	Gawking at an accident
Extending an apology (where appropriate)	Using sarcasm
Picking up litter	Mimicking
Planting a flower	Forgetting a birthday
Waiting your turn	Blowing your car horn
Holding a door	Talking with your mouth full
Extending a hand	Playing with your nose
Congratulating someone	Eating loudly
Sharing a poem	Showing lack of concern
Remembering important occasions	Sneering
Sharing a sandwich	Being late
Using a napkin	Staring at someone
Offering someone a chair	Littering
Bringing flowers	Shoving ahead of others
Playing a game together	Stamping your foot
Expressing regret	Telling a lie
Waving with both hands	Dumping ashtrays in the street
Giving a thumbs-up sign	Insulting a person
Overlooking a faux pas	Talking during a program

Physical Environments

Forty Inviting Qualities	Forty Disinviting Qualities
Fresh paint	Dark corridors
Pleasant smells	Bad smells
Living plants	Dingy colors
Attractive, up-to-date bulletin boards	Full trash cans
Soft lighting	Hard lighting
Big and soft pillows	Insects (flies, roaches)
Lots of books	Excessive noise
Fresh air	Smoke-filled room
Fireplace	Bare walls
Comfortable furniture	Leftover food
Rocking chair	Dirty coffee cups
Flowers on the desk	Full ashtrays
Open doors	Bare lightbulb
Candy jar with candy	Stack of out-of-date materials
Soft music	Fluorescent lights that buzz
Attractive pictures	Dark parking lots
Comfortable temperature	Full pencil sharpener
Cup of coffee, tea, or juice	Dead plants
Porch light at night	Long lines
Porch swing	Dingy curtains
Birthday cake	Burned-out lightbulbs
Fresh towels	Sidewalks going where people don't
Well-tended park	Opaque windows
Books and magazines	Cold room
Stuffed animals	Lukewarm coffee
Sunny room	Artificial plants and flowers
Game board	Cigarette butts on a plate
Thick carpet	Sink full of dirty dishes
This morning's paper	Exhaust fumes
Holiday tree	Straight rows
Matching colors	Empty mail box
Birthday card	Dirty fingerprints
Positively worded signs	Peeling paint and plaster
Blue jeans and cotton shirts	Nothing to read
Bright hallways	Dusty, cobwebby shelves
Clean aromas	Stuffy room
Brightly lit parking lot	Sticky floors
Clean windows	Broken windows
Clear floors	Signs with letters missing
Old pick-up truck	Spray-painted graffiti

Printed Signs

Forty Inviting Signs

Please Use Sidewalks
Welcome
Visitor Parking
Please Leave Message
Open, Come In
No Appointment Necessary
Please Use Other Door
Thank You for Not Smoking
Come Back Soon
Open House
We're Glad You're Here
Handicapped Parking
Sorry I Missed You, Please Come Back
Visitors Welcome
Happy Hour
Please Put Litter Here
Come As You Are
Open to the Public
Rest Area
Take Me
Clean Restrooms
Help Keep North Carolina Beautiful
Library
Have Lunch with Us
Students Welcome Back
Please Excuse the Inconvenience
Good Day
Happy Holidays
No Waiting
You're Here
Please Touch
Come On In
Pardon Our Dust
Ample Parking in the Rear
May We Help You?
Be Back at _____
Please Watch Your Step
Help Us Conserve Energy
Directory Assistance
Welcome to Canada

Forty Disinviting Signs

Office Closed
Do Not Disturb
Keep off Grass
No Trespassing
No Talking
No Running in Halls
No Admission without Pass
No Admittance
Visitors Must Report to _____
No Smoking
Be Seated
Keep Out
Do Not Enter
No Deposit
No Return
Tow Zone
By Appointment Only
Out of Order
Beware of the Dog
No Children Allowed
Closed to the Public
Private Beach
No Checks Cashed
No Spitting on Sidewalk
Members Only
For Faculty Use Only
We Do Not Give Change
Take a Number and Wait
Shoplifters Will Be Prosecuted: This Means You!
Keep This Door *Shut!*
Stay in line
Not for Public Use
Out to Lunch
You Broke It, You Bought It
Books Are for Sale Only
Government Property—No Admittance
Do Not Remove under Penalty of Law
Restrooms for Customers Only
Parking for Officials Only
Do Not Touch This TV
No Facilities

References

Adelman, H.S. & Taylor, L. (1993). *Learning problems and learning disabilities: Moving forward.* Pacific Grove, CA: Brooks/Cole.

Albert, L. (1989). *A teacher's guide to cooperative discipline.* Circle Pines, MN: American Guidance Service.

Alberti, R.E. & Emmons, M.L. (1990). *Your perfect right.* San Louis Obispo, CA: Impact Publishers.

Allport, G.W. (1937). *Personality: A psychological interpretation.* New York: Holt, Rinehart & Winston.

Allport, G.W. (1943). The ego in contemporary psychology. *Psychological Review, 50,* 451–478.

Allport, G.W. (1955). *Becoming.* New Haven: Yale University Press.

Allport, G.W. (1961). *Pattern and growth in personality.* New York: Holt, Rinehart & Winston.

American Association of University Women. (1991). *Shortchanging girls, shortchanging America.* A nationwide poll to assess self esteem, educational experiences, interest in math and science, and career aspirations of girls and boys ages 9–15. Washington, DC.

Amos, L. (1985). *Professionally and personally inviting teacher practices as related to affective course outcomes reported by dental hygiene students.* Unpublished doctoral dissertation, The University of North Carolina at Greensboro.

Anderson, W.T. (1990). *Reality isn't what it used to be: Theoretical politics, ready to wear religion, global myths, primitive chic, and other wonders of the post-modern world.* San Francisco: Harper.

Apple, M. (1987). *Teachers are texts: A political economy of class and gender relations in education.* Boston: Routledge & Kegan Paul.

Arceneaux, C.J. (1994). Trust: An exploration of its nature and significance. *Journal of Invitational Theory and Practice, 3,* 35–49.

Arnold, V. & Roach, T. (1989). Teaching: A nonverbal communication event. *Business Education Forum, 44,* 18–20.

Avila, D. & Purkey, W.W. (1966). Intrinsic and extrinsic motivation: A regrettable distinction. *Psychology in the Schools, 3,* 206–210.

Bandura, A. (1986). *Social foundations of thought and action: A social cognitive theory.* Englewood Cliffs, NJ: Prentice-Hall.

Barron, D.D. (1992). They're back! Invite them in. *School-Library-Media Activities Monthly, 9* (1), 48–50.

Beane, J.A. (1990). *Affect in the curriculum: Toward democracy, dignity and diversity.* New York: Teachers College Press.

Beane, J.A. (1991). Sorting out the self-esteem controversy. *Educational Leadership, 49,* 25–30.

Benedict, G.C. (1990). The Affton School District experience. In W.W. Purkey & J.J. Schmidt (Eds.), *Invitational learning for counseling and development* (pp. 89–100). Ann Arbor, MI: ERIC/CAPS.

Bennett, A.C. & Novak, J.M. (1981, April). *Looking for the inviting and just school environment.* Paper presented at the meeting of the American Educational Research Association, Los Angeles, CA.

Bennett, J. (1982). *Regrets and prides: Invitations accepted or not accepted.* Unpublished paper, The University of North Carolina at Greensboro.

Bennis, W. & Nanus, B. (1985). *Leaders: The strategies for taking charge.* New York: Harper & Row.

Berger, P. & Luckman, T. (1966). *The social construction of reality: A treatise in the sociology of knowledge.* Garden City, NY: Doubleday.

Bergman, K. & Gaitskill, T. (1990). Faculty and student perceptions of effective clinical teachers. *Journal of Professional Nursing, 6* (1) 33–44.

Berman, S. & LaForge, P. (Eds.). (1993). *Promising practices in teaching social responsibility.* Albany: State University of New York Press.

Biklen, S.K. & Pollard, D. (Eds.), (1993) *Gender and education ninety-second yearbook of the national society for the study of education: Part I.* Chicago: University of Chicago.

Bingham, R.D., Haubrich, P.A., White, S.B. & Zipp, J.F. (1990). Dual standards among teachers: This school is good enough for other kids but not my child. *Urban Education, 25,* 274–288.

Blackburn, J. (1990). The Sugar Loaf School experience. In W.W. Purkey & J.J. Schmidt (Eds.), *Invitational learning for counseling and development* (pp. 111–118). Ann Arbor, MI: ERIC/CAPS.

Bloom, B.S. (1976). *Human characteristics and school learning.* New York: McGraw-Hill.

Bogdan, R.C. & Biklen, S.K. (1992). *Qualitative research for education: An introduction to theory and methods* (2nd ed). Boston: Allyn & Bacon.

Branch, C. (1974). *An investigation of inferred and professed self-concepts-as-learner of disruptive and nondisruptive middle school students.* Unpublished doctoral dissertation, University of Florida.

Branch, C., Damico, S. & Purkey, W.W. (1977). A comparison between the self-concepts-as-learner of disruptive and nondisruptive middle school students. *The Middle School Journal, 7,* 15–16.

Brophy, J.E. (1983). Classroom organization and management. *Elementary School Journal, 83,* 265–285.

Brophy, J.E. (1987). Synthesis of research on strategies for motivating students to learn. *Educational Leadership, 45,* 40–48.

Brown, C. (1965). *Manchild in the promised land.* New York: Macmillan.

Brubaker, D. (1994). *Creative curriculum leadership.* Thousand Oaks, CA: Corwin Press.

Buber, M. (1965). *The knowledge of man: Selected essays.* New York: Harper & Row.

Byrne, B.M. (1984). The general/academic self-concept nomological network: A review of construct validation research. *Review of Educational Research, 54,* 427–456.

Byrne, B.M. (1986). Self-concept/academic achievement relations: An investigation of dimensionality, stability and causality. *Canadian Journal of Behavioral Science, 18,* 173–186.

Byrne, B.M., Shavelson, R.J. & Marsh, H.W. (1992). Multigroup comparisons in self-concept research: Reexamining the assumption of equivalent structure and measurement. In T.M. Brinthaupt & R.P. Lipka (Eds.). *The self-definitional and methodological issues.* (pp. 172–203). Albany: State University of New York Press.

Calderhead, K. & Robson, M. (1991). Images of teaching: Student teachers' early conceptions of classroom practice. *Teaching & Teacher Education, 7,* 1–8.

Canfield, J. & Wells, H. (1976). *100 Ways to enhance self-concept in the classroom: A handbook for teachers and parents.* Englewood Cliffs, NJ: Prentice-Hall.

Carnegie Foundation for the Advancement of Teaching. (1991). *The condition of teaching: A state-by-state analysis.* Washington, DC: The Carnegie Foundation.

Carroll, L. (1971). *Alice in wonderland.* New York: W.W. Norton.

Cartwright, D.S., Tomson, B., & Schwartz, H. (Eds.). (1975). *Gang delinquency.* Monterey, CA: Brooks/Cole.

Chance, D. (1990). The East Davidson experience. In W.W. Purkey & J.J. Schmidt (Eds.), *Invitational learning for counseling and development* (pp. 71–78). Ann Arbor, MI: ERIC/CAPS.

Chance, D. (1992). *A study of five diverse middle schools and their efforts to bring about positive changes with "at risk" students through invitational education.* Unpublished doctoral dissertation, The University of North Carolina at Greensboro.

Chapman, J.W. (1988). Learning disabled children's self concept. *Review of Educational Research, 58,* 347–371.

Charles, C.M. (1981). *Building classroom discipline: From models to practice.* New York: Longman.

Childs, J.L. (1931). *Education and the philosophy of experimentalism.* New York: Century.

Clark, C.M. (1988). Asking the right questions about teacher preparation: Contributions of research on teaching thinking. *Educational Researcher, 17* (2) 5–12.

Clark, C.M. & Peterson, P.L. (1986). Teacher thought processes. In M.C. Wittrock (Ed.). *Handbook of research on teaching* (3rd ed., pp. 255–296). New York: Macmillan.

Clifford, M.M. (1990). Students need challenge, not easy success. *Educational Leadership, 48* (1), 22–26.

Colangelo, N., Kelly, K.R. & Schrepfer, R.M. (1987). A comparison of gifted, general, and special learning needs of students' academic and social self-concept. *Journal of Counseling and Development, 66,* 73–77.

Cole, A.L. (1989, April). *Making explicit implicit theories of teaching: Starting points in preservice programs.* Paper presented at the Annual Meeting of the American Educational Research Association, San Francisco.

Combs, A.W. (Ed.). (1962). *Perceiving, behaving, becoming.* Washington, DC: Yearbook of the Association for Supervision and Curriculum Development.

Combs, A.W. (1982). *A personal approach to teaching: Beliefs that make a difference.* Boston: Allyn & Bacon.

Combs, A.W. (1989). *A theory of therapy: Guidelines for counseling practice.* Newbury Park, CA: Sage Publications.

Combs, A.W., Avila, D. & Purkey, W.W. (1978). *Helping relationships: Basic concepts for the helping professions* (2nd ed.). Boston: Allyn & Bacon.

Combs, A.W., Blume, R.A., Newman, A.J. & Wass, H.L. (1974). *The professional education of teachers: A humanistic approach to teacher preparation* (2nd ed.). Boston: Allyn & Bacon.

Combs, A.W. & Gonzalez, D.M. (1994). *Helping Relationships: Basic concepts for the helping professions* (4th ed.). Boston: Allyn & Bacon.

Combs, A.W., Richards, A.C. & Richards, F. (1976). *Perceptual psychology: A humanistic approach to the study of persons.* New York: Harper & Row.

Combs, A. W. & Snygg, D. (1959). *Individual behavior: A perceptual approach to behavior* (2nd ed.). New York: Harper & Row.

Combs, A.W., Soper, D.W., Gooding, C.T., Benton, J.A., Jr., Dickman, J.F. & Usher, R.H. (1969). *Florida studies in the helping professions.* (Social Science Monograph No. 37). Gainesville: University of Florida Press.

Coopersmith, S. (1967). *The antecedents of self-esteem.* San Francisco: W.H. Freeman.

Cotler, S.B. & Guerra, J.J. (1976). *Assertion training: A humanistic behavioral guide to self-dignity.* Champaign, IL: Research Press.

Covington, M.V. (1984). The motive for self-worth. In R.A. Mes and C. Ames (Eds.) *Research in education: Student motivation* (pp. 77–113). Orlando, FL: Academic Press.

Csikszentmihalyi, M. (1990). *Flow: The psychology of optimal experience.* New York: Harcourt Brace Jovanovich.

Csikszentmihalyi, M. (1993). *The evolving self: A psychology for the third millennium.* New York: HarperCollins.

Curwin, R.L. & Mendler, A.N. (1988). *Discipline with Dignity.* Alexandria, VA: Association for Supervision and Curriculum Development.

Darakjian, G.P., Michael, W.P. & Knapp-Lee, L. (1985). The long-term predictive validity of an academic self-concept measure relative to criterion of secondary school grades earned over eleven semesters. *Educational and Psychological Measurement, 45,* 397–400.

Deci, E.L. & Ryan, R.M. (1987). The support for autonomy and the control of behaviour. *Journal of Personality and Social Psychology, 53*, 1024–1037.

Denzin, N.K. (1989). *Interpretive interactionism.* Newbury Park, CA: Sage Publications.

Dewey, J. (1916). *Democracy and education.* New York: Macmillan.

Dewey, J. (1930). *Individualism old and new.* New York: Minton, Balch & Company.

Dewey, J. (1933). *How we think.* Lexington, MA: D.C. Heath.

Diggory, J.C. (1966). *Self-evaluation: Concepts and studies.* New York: John Wiley.

Dorland's Illustrated Medical Dictionary (25th ed.) (1974). Philadelphia: W.B. Saunders.

Dreikurs, R. & Cassel, P. (1974). *Discipline without tears.* New York: Hawthorne.

Dumas, A. (1844/1962). *The three musketeers.* New York: Macmillan.

Eccles, J.S. & Midgley, C. (1989). State-environment fit: Developmentally appropriate classrooms for young adolescents. In C. Ames & R. Ames (Eds.) *Motivation in education* (pp. 139–186). San Diego: Academic Press.

Edelman, M. (1985). The sea is so wide and my boat is so small: Problems facing Black children today. In H.P. McAdoo & J.L. McAdoo (Eds.) *Black children: Social, educational, and parental environments* (pp. 72–82). Beverly Hills, CA: Sage Publications.

Edelwich, J. (with Brodsky, A.). (1980). *Burnout: Stages of disillusionment in the helping professions.* New York: Human Sciences Press.

Egan, G. (1990). *The skilled helper* (4th ed.) Pacific Grove, CA: Brooks/Cole.

Eisner, E.W. (1991). *The enlightened eye: Qualitative inquiry and the enhancement of educational practice.* New York: Macmillan.

Elkind, D. (1981). *The hurried child: Growing up too fast too soon.* Reading, MA: Addison-Wesley.

Eshel, Y., & Klein, Z. (1981). Development of academic self-concept of lower-class primary school children. *Journal of Educational Psychology, 73*, 287–293.

Esquiriel, L. (1992). *Like water for chocolate.* New York: Doubleday (English Translation).

Fenstermacher, G.D. (1986). Philosophy of research on teaching: Three aspects. In M.C. Wittrock (Ed.). *Handbook of research on teaching.* (3rd ed., pp. 37–49). New York: Macmillan.

Finger, J.P.K. (1995). *A study of professional and inferred self-concept-as-learner of male African American middle grade students.* Unpublished doctoral dissertation, University of North Carolina, Greensboro.

Fink, D. (1992). Invitational leadership. In J.M. Novak (Ed.), *Advancing invitational thinking* (pp. 137–156). San Francisco: Caddo Gap Press.

Fisher, R. & Ury, W. (1981). *Getting to yes: Negotiating agreement without giving in.* Boston: Houghton Mifflin.

Fitts, W.H. & Hamner, W.T. (1969). *The self-concept and delinquency* (Nashville Mental Health Center Monograph No. 1). Nashville: Counselor Recordings and Tests.

Friedman, H. & Friedman, P. (1973). *Frequency and types of teacher reinforcement given to lower- and middle-class students.* Paper presented at the meeting of the American Educational Research Association, New Orleans.

Fromm, E. (1947). *Man for himself.* New York: Rinehart.

Fuqua, D., Newman, J., Anderson, M. & Johnson, A. (1986). Preliminary study of internal dialogue in a training session. *Psychological Reports, 58,* 163–172.

Fullan, M. (1991). *The new meaning of educational change.* Toronto: OISE Press.

Galbo, J. (1989). The teacher as significant other: A review of the literature. *Adolescence, 24,* 549–556.

Gardner, H. (1991). *The unschooled mind: How children think and how schools should teach.* New York: Basic Books

Gathercoal, F. (1991). *Judicious discipline.* San Francisco: Caddo Gap Press.

Gerber, T. (1982, March). *The young adolescent: Invitations to school success.* Paper presented at the meeting of the American Educational Research Association Convention, New York.

Gilligan, C. (1982). *In a different voice.* Cambridge, MA: Harvard University Press.

Gilligan, C., Lyons, N.P. & Hammer, T.J. (1990). *Making connections.* Cambridge, MA: Harvard University Press.

Gilligan, C., Ward, J.V. & Taylor, J.M. (1988). *Mapping the moral domain.* Cambridge, MA: Harvard University Press.

Glenn, C.L. (1992, November). Debates in education resolved: Enhancing pupil self-esteem should be a major priority of schools. *Curriculum Review,* 4–6.

Goffin, S. (1989). How well do we respect the children in our care? *Childhood Education, 66,* 68–74.

Goldman, L. (1989). Moving counseling research into the twenty-first century. *The Counseling Psychologist, 17,* 81–85.

Good, T.L. (1980). *Teacher influence and student influence: A brief comment* (Technical Report No. 221, Center for Research in Social Behavior). Columbia: University of Missouri.

Good, T.L. (1981). Teacher expectations and student perceptions: A decade of research. *Educational Leadership, 38* (5), 415–422.

Good, T.L., Biddle, B.J. & Brophy, J.E. (1975). *Teachers make a difference.* New York: Holt, Rinehart & Winston.

Good, T.L. & Brophy, J.E. (1977). *Educational psychology: A realistic approach.* New York: Holt, Rinehart & Winston.

Good, T.L. & Brophy, J.E. (1978). *Looking in classrooms* (2nd ed.). New York: Harper & Row.

Good, T.L & Brophy, J.E. (1994). *Looking in classrooms* (6th ed.). New York: HarperCollins College Publishers.

Goodman, J. (1988). Constructing a practical philosophy of teaching: A study of preservice teachers' professional perspectives. *Teaching & Teacher Education, 4,* 121–137.

Gordon, T. (1974). *T.E.T.: Teacher-effectiveness training.* New York: Peter H. Wyden.

Graham, S. (1994). Motivation in African Americans. *Review of Educational Research, 64*, 55–117.

Graves, W.H. (1972). *A multivariate investigation of professed and inferred self concepts of fifth and sixth grade students.* Unpublished doctoral dissertation, University of Florida, Gainesville.

Gregory, D. (1964). *Nigger.* New York: Simon & Schuster.

Griffore, R.J. & Bianchi, L. (1984). Effects of ordinal position on academic self-concept. *Psychological Reports, 55,* 263–268.

Guba, E.G. (Ed.). (1990). *The paradigm dialogue.* Newbury Park, CA: Sage Publications.

Guskey, T.R. (1986). Staff development and the process of teacher change. *Educational Researcher, 15* (5), 5–12.

Haberman, M. (1994). Gentle teaching in a violent society. *Educational Horizons.* 72–73, 131–136.

Hansford, B.C. & Hattie, J.A. (1982). The relationship between self and achievement/performance. *Review of Educational Research, 52,* 123–142.

Harper, K., & Purkey, W.W. (1993). Self-concept-as-learner of middle level students. *Research in Middle Level Education, 17,* 80–89.

Harter, S. (1983). Developmental perspectives on the self-system. In P.H. Mussen (Ed.) *Handbook of child psychology,* Vol. 4, pp. 275–385.

Harter, S., (1988). Causes, correlates, and the functional role of global self-worth: A life-span perspective. In *Perceptions of competence and incompetence across the life span.* In J. Kolligian and R. Sternberg, (Eds). New Haven: Yale University Press.

Hattie, J.A. (1992). *Self-Concept.* Hillsdale, NJ: Lawrence Erlbaum Associates.

Hoge, R.D. & Renzulli, J.S. (1993). Exploring the link between giftedness and self-concept. *Review of Educational Research, 63,* 449–465.

Holt, J. (1982). *How children fail.* New York: Delta/Seymour Lawrence Publishing.

Hook, S. (1939). *John Dewey: An intellectual portrait.* New York: John Day.

House, J.D. (1992). The relationship between perceived task competence, achievement expectancies, and school withdrawal of academically underprepared adolescent students. *Child Study Journal, 22,* 4, 253–272.

Hull, J. & Young, R. (1993). The self-awareness-reducing effects of alcohol: Evidence and implications. In J. Suls & A. Greenwald (Eds.), *Psychological perspectives on the self* (Vol. 2) (159–190). Hillsdale, NJ: Lawrence Erlbaum Associates.

Hunt, J.M. (1961). *Intelligence and experience.* New York: Ronald Press.

Inglis, S.C. (1976). *The development and validation of an instrument to assess teacher invitations and teacher effectiveness as reported by students in a technical and general post-secondary setting.* Unpublished doctoral dissertation, University of Florida, Gainesville.

Insel, P. & Jacobson, L. (1975). *What do you expect? An inquiry into self-fulfilling prophecies.* Menlo Park, CA: Cummings.

Ivey, A. (1977). Cultural expertise: Toward systematic outcome criteria in counseling and psychological education. *Personnel and Guidance Journal, 55,* 296–302.

James, W. (1890). *Principles of psychology* (2 vols.). New York: Henry Holt.

Janesick, V. (1977). *An ethnographic study of a teacher's classroom perspective.* Unpublished doctoral dissertation, Michigan State University, East Lansing.

Johnson, D.W. (1993). *Reaching out: Interpersonal effectiveness and self-actualization* (5th ed.). Boston: Allyn & Bacon.

Johnson, D.W. & Johnson, R.T. (1989). *Leading the cooperative school.* Edina, MN: Interaction Book Co.

Jones, S.C. & Panitch, D. (1971). The self-fulfilling prophecy and interpersonal attraction. *Journal of Experimental Social Psychology, 7,* 356–366.

Jourard, S.M. (1964). *The transparent self: Self-disclosure and well-being.* Princeton, NJ: Van Nostrand.

Jourard, S.M. (Ed.). (1967). *To be or not to be: Existential psychological perspectives on the self.* Tallahassee: Board of Commissioners of State Institutions of Florida.

Jourard, S.M. (1968). *Disclosing man to himself.* Princeton, NJ: Van Nostrand.

Jourard, S.M. (1971). *Self-disclosure: An experimental analysis of the transparent self.* New York: Wiley-Interscience.

Jourard, S.M. (1974). *The undisclosed self.* New York: Mentor Books.

Kagan, D.M. (1992). Implications of research on teacher belief. *Educational Psychologist, 27,* 65–90.

Kegan, R. (1982). *The evolving self: Problem and process in human development.* Cambridge, MA: Harvard University Press.

Kelly, G.A. (1955). *The psychology of personal constructs* (Vols. 1 & 2). New York: W.W. Norton.

Kelly, K.R. & Jordan, L. (1990) Effects of academic achievement and gender on academic and social self-concept: A replication study. *Journal of Counseling and Development, 69,* 173–177.

Kendall, P.C., Howard, B. & Hays, R. (1989). Self-referent speech and psychopathology: The balance of positive and negative thinking. *Cognitive Therapy and Research, 13,* 583–598.

Klein, S.B. & Ortman, P.E. (1994). Continuing the journey toward gender equity. *Educational Researcher, 23* (8), 13–21.

Knowles, J. H. (1977). The responsibility of the individual. In J. H. Knowles (Ed.). *Doing better and feeling worse: Health in the United States.* New York: W.W. Norton.

Kohlberg, L. (1969). Stage and sequence: The cognitive-developmental approach to socialization. In D.A. Goslin (Ed.), *Handbook of socialization theory and research.* Chicago: Rand McNally.

Kohlberg, L. & Turiel, E. (1971). *Research in moral development: The cognitive developmental approach.* New York: Holt, Rinehart & Winston.

Kongshem, G. (1992). Securing your schools: Are metal detectors the answer? *The Executive Educator, 14* (6), 30–31.

Kraft, A. (1975). *The living classroom: Putting humanistic education into practice.* New York: Harper & Row.

Kruglanski, A., Stein, C. & Riter, A. (1977). Contingencies of exogenous reward and task performance: On the minimax strategy in instrumental behaviour. *Journal of Applied Social Psychology, 2,* 141–148.

Krumboltz, J.D. (1986). Research is a very good thing. *The Counseling Psychologist, 14,* 159–163.

Kupfer, J.H. (1983). *Experience as art: Aesthetics in everyday life.* Albany: State University of New York Press.

Lambeth, C.R. (1980). *Teacher invitations and effectiveness as reported by secondary students in Virginia.* Unpublished doctoral dissertation, University of Virginia, Charlottesville.

Lappé, F.M. & Du Bois, P.M. (1994). *The quickening of America: Rebuilding our nation, remaking our lives.* San Francisco: Jossey-Bass.

Lecky, P. (1945). *Self-consistency: A theory of personality.* New York: Island Press.

Lehr, J. (1990). The Furman University Center for Excellence experience. In W.W. Purkey & J.J. Schmidt (Eds.), *Invitational learning for counseling and development* (pp. 63–70). Ann Arbor, MI: ERIC/CAPS.

Lepper, M.R. & Greene, D. (1975). Turning play into work: Effects of adult surveillance and extrinsic rewards on children's intrinsic motivation. *Journal of Personality and Social Psychology, 31,* 479–486.

Lepper, M.R. & Hodell, M. (1989). Intrinsic motivation in the classroom. In C. Ames & R. Ames (Eds.), *Motivation in education* (pp. 73–106). San Diego, CA: Academic Press.

Lezotte, L.W. (1989, August). Base school improvement on what we know about effective schools. *The American School Board Journal,* 18–20.

Lezotte, L.W. (1990). *Workbook for developing a district plan for school improvement.* Okemos, MI: Effective School Products.

Lichtenberg, J.W. (1986). Counseling research: Irrelevant or ignored? *Journal of Counseling and Development, 64,* 365–366.

Lickona, T. (1991). *Educating for character: How our school can teach respect and responsibility.* New York: Bantam.

Liebman, J.L. (1946). *Peace of mind.* New York: Simon & Schuster.

Lippitt, R. & White, R. (1960). *Autocracy and democracy.* New York: Harper.

Maehr, M. (1974). *Sociocultural origins of achievement.* Monterey, CA: Brooks/Cole.

Mahon, R. & Altman, H. (1977). Skill training: Cautions and recommendations. *Counselor Education and Supervision, 17* (1), 42–50.

Mahoney, M.J. (1975). The sensitive scientist in empirical humanism. *American Psychologist, 30,* 864–867.

Manning, J. (1959). Discipline in the good old days. *Phi Delta Kappan, 41* (3), 87–91.

Markus, H. & Wurf, E. (1987). The dynamic self-concept: A social psychological analysis. In M. Rosenzweig & L. Porter (Eds.), *Annual review of psychology* (Vol. 48, pp. 299–338). Palo Alto, CA: Annual Reviews.

Marquez, G.G. (1988). *Love in the time of cholera.* New York: Alfred A. Knopf.

Marsh, H.W. (1993). The multidimensional structure of academic self-concept: Invariance over gender and age. *American Educational Research Journal, 30,* 841–860.

Masters, E.L. (1922). *Spoon River anthology.* New York: Macmillan.

Matthews, D.B. (1991). The effects of school environment on intrinsic motivation of middle-school children. *Journal of Humanistic Education and Development, 30,* 30–36.

McAdoo, H.P. & McAdoo, J.L. (1985). *Black children: Social, educational, and parental environments.* Beverly Hills, CA: Sage Publications.

McBrien, D.E. (1990). The Baltimore County Guidance experience. In W.W. Purkey & J.J. Schmidt (Eds.), *Invitational learning for counseling and development* (pp. 53–62). Ann Arbor, MI: ERIC/CAPS.

Mead, G. H. (1934). *Mind, self and society.* Chicago: University of Chicago Press.

Meichenbaum, D. (1974). *Cognitive behavior modification.* Morristown, NJ: General Learning Press.

Meichenbaum, D. (1977). *Cognitive behaviour modification: An integrative approach.* New York: Plenum Press.

Meichenbaum, D. (1985). *Stress inoculation training.* New York: Pergamon.

Mezzacappa, D. (1993, June 12). Clinton wants funds to fight growing violence in schools. *The Atlanta Journal/The Atlantic Constitution,* p. A5.

Moustakas, C.E. (1966). *The authentic teacher: Sensitivity and awareness in the classroom.* Cambridge, MA: Howard A. Doyle.

Moustakas, C.E. (1990). *Heuristic research: Design, methodology, and application.* Newbury Park, CA: Sage Publications.

NEA (1993, January 11). *Now: A weekly newsletter.* Washington, DC: National Education Association.

Nespor, J. (1987). The roles of beliefs in the practice of teaching. *Journal of Curriculum Studies, 19,* 317–328.

Noddings, N. (1984). *Caring: A feminine approach to ethics and moral education.* Berkeley: University of California Press.

Noddings, N. (1986). Fidelity in teaching, teacher education, and research for teaching. *Harvard Educational Review, 54* (4), 496–510.

Noddings, N. (1992). *The challenge to care in schools: An alternative approach to education.* New York: Teachers College Press.

Noddings, N. (1993). *Educating for intelligent belief or unbelief.* New York: Teachers College Press.

Novak, J.M. (1990). Advancing constructive education: A constructive framework for teacher education. In G.J. Neimeyer & R.A. Neimeyer (Eds.), *Advances in personal construct psychology* (pp. 233–255). Greenwich, CT: JAI Press.

Novak, J.M. (1991). Grounding invitational teaching: A theory of practice perspective. *Brock Education, 1* (2), 8–12.

Novak, J.M. (Ed.). (1992a). *Advancing invitational thinking.* San Francisco: Caddo Gap Press.

Novak, J.M. (1992b). Critical imagination for invitational theory, research, and practice. *Journal of Invitational Theory and Practice, 1* (2), 77–86.

Novak, J.M. (1994). The talk and walk of democratic teacher education. In J.M. Novak (Ed.), *Democratic teacher education: Programs, processes, problems and prospects* (pp. 1–6). Albany: State University of New York Press.

Nozick, R. (1989). *The examined life: Philosophical meditations.* New York: Simon & Schuster.

O'Roark, A.M. (1974). *A comparison of the perceptual characteristics of elected legislators and public school counselors identified as most and least effective.* Unpublished doctoral dissertation, University of Florida.

Ouchi, W.G. (1981). *Theory Z: How American business can meet the Japanese challenge.* Reading, MA: Addison-Wesley.

Owen, E.H. (1972). *A comparison of disadvantaged and non-disadvantaged elementary school pupils on two measures of self-concept as learner.* Unpublished doctoral dissertation, University of Florida.

Pajares, M.F. (1992). Teachers' beliefs and educational research: Cleaning up a messy construct. *Review of Educational Research, 62* (3) 307–332.

Patterson, C.H. (1961). The self in recent Rogerian theory. *Journal of Individual Psychology, 17,* 5–11.

Patterson, C.H. (1973). *Humanistic education.* Englewood Cliffs, NJ: Prentice-Hall.

Patterson, C.H. & Purkey, W.W. (1993). The preparation of humanistic teachers for schools of the next century. *Journal of Humanistic Education and Development, 30,* 147–155.

Piaget, J. (1973). *The child's conception of the world.* London, GB: Paladin.

Pintrich, P.R. (1990). Implications of psychological research on student learning and college teaching for teacher education. In W.R. Houston (Ed.), *Handbook of research on teacher education* (pp. 826–857). New York: Macmillan.

Plum, A. (1981). Communication as skill: A critique and alternative proposal. *Journal of Humanistic Psychology, 21* (4), 3–19.

Postman, N. (1993). *Technology: The surrender of culture to technology.* New York: Vintage Books.

Powers, W.T. (1973). *Behavior: The control of perception.* Chicago: Aldine.

Prillaman, A.R., Eaker, D.J. & Kendrick, D.M. (Eds.). (1994). *The tapestry of caring: Education as nurturance.* Norwood, NJ: Ablex Publishing.

Purkey, W.W. (1978). *Inviting school success: A self-concept approach to teaching and learning.* Belmont, CA: Wadsworth.

Purkey, W.W., Cage, B. & Graves, W.H. (1973). The Florida Key: A scale to infer learner self-concept. *Journal of Educational and Psychological Measurement, 33*, 979–984.

Purkey, W.W. & Novak, J.M. (1984). *Inviting school success: A self-concept approach to teaching and learning* (2nd ed.). Belmont, CA: Wadsworth.

Purkey, W.W. & Novak, J.M. (1988). *Education: By invitation only* (Fastback #268). Bloomington, IN: Phi Delta Kappa.

Purkey, W.W. & Novak, J.M. (1993). The Invitational Helix: A systemic guide for individual and organizational development. *Journal of Invitational Theory and Practice, 2–2*, 59–67.

Purkey, W.W. & Schmidt, J.J. (1996). *Invitational Counseling: A Self-Concept Approach to Professional Practice.* Monterey, CA: Brooks/Cole.

Purkey, W.W. & Stanley, P.H. (1994). *The inviting school treasury: 1001 ways to invite student success.* New York: Scholastic.

Purkey, W.W. & Strahan, D.B. (1986). *Positive discipline: A pocketful of ideas.* Columbus, OH: National Middle School Association.

Purkey, W.W., Strahan, D.B., Corders, R. & Lucas, R. (1994). *Invitational education: A fresh strategy for school success.* Unpublished paper, The University of North Carolina at Greensboro, NC.

Quarles, C.L. (1989). *School violence: A survival guide for school staff with emphasis on robbery, rape and hostage taking.* Washington, DC: NEA Professional Library.

Radd, T.R. (1988). *The effects of Grow with Guidance on self-concept-as-learner and teacher self-concept.* Unpublished doctoral dissertation, University of Akron, Akron, OH.

Raimy, V.C. (1948). Self-reference in counseling interviews. *Journal of Consulting Psychology, 12*, 153–163.

Reed, C. (1992). Invitation and multicultural perspectives. In J.M. Novak (Ed.), *Advancing invitational thinking* (pp. 47–76). San Francisco: Caddo Gap Press.

Riley, J.W. (1916). *James Whitcomb Riley's Complete Works* (Vol. 5). New York: Bobbs-Merrill.

Ripley, D.M. (1985). *Invitational teaching behaviors in the associate degree clinical setting.* Unpublished master's thesis, School of Nursing, University of North Carolina, Greensboro.

Robertiello, R. & Schoenewolf, G. (1987). *101 common therapeutic blunders.* Northvale, NJ: Aronson.

Roderick, M. (1994). Grade retention and school dropout: Investigating the association. *American Educational Research Journal, 31* (4), 729–759.

Rogers, C.R. (1947). Some observations on the organization of personality. *American Psychologist, 2*, 358–368.

Rogers, C.R. (1951). *Client-centered therapy.* Boston: Houghton Mifflin.

Rogers, C.R. (1959). *Counseling and psychotherapy: Theory and practice.* New York: Harper & Row.

Rogers, C.R. (1965). The therapeutic relationship: Recent theory and research. *Australian Journal of Psychology, 17* (2), 95–108.

Rogers, C.R. (1967). *Coming into existence.* New York: World.

Rogers, C.R. (1969). *Freedom to learn.* Columbus, OH: Charles E. Merrill.

Rogers, C.R. (1973). My philosophy of interpersonal relationships and how it grew. *Journal of Humanistic Psychology, 13* (2), 12–19.

Rogers, C.R. (1974). In retrospect—Forty-six years. *American Psychologist, 29* (2), 115.

Rogers, C. R. (1980). *A way of being.* Boston: Houghton Mifflin.

Rosenberg, M.J. (1979). *Conceiving the self.* New York: Basic Books.

Rowe, M.B. (1974a). Relation of wait-time and rewards to the development of language, logic and fate control. Part II—Rewards. *Journal of Research in Science Teaching, 11* (4) 290–308.

Rowe, M.B. (1974b). Wait-time and rewards as instructional variables, their influence on language, logic, and fate-control. Part I—Wait-time. *Journal of Research in Science Teaching, 2* (2), 81–94.

Saint-Exupéry, A. de. (1943). *The little prince.* New York: Harcourt, Brace & World.

Scheffler, I. (1985). *Of human potential: An essay in the philosophy of education.* Boston: Routledge & Kegan Paul.

Schmidt, J.J. (1984). Counselor intentionality: An emerging view of process and performance. *Journal of Counseling Psychology, 31,* 383–386.

Schmidt, J.J. (1994). *Living intentionally and making life happen* (Rev. ed.). Greenville, NC: Brookcliff.

Schmoker, M. (1990, March). Sentimentalizing self-esteem. *The Education Digest,* 55–56.

Schommer, M. (1990). Effects of beliefs about the nature of knowledge on comprehension. *Journal of Educational Psychology, 82,* 498–504.

Schrag, F. (1995). *Back to basics: Fundamental educational questions reexamined.* San Francisco: Jossey-Bass.

Schunk, D.H. (1984). The self-efficacy perspective on achievement behavior. *Educational Psychologist, 19,* 119–218.

Schunk, D.H. (1989). Social cognitive theory and self-regulating learning. In B.J. Zimmerman & D.H. Schunk (Eds.), *Self-regulated learning and academic achievement: Theory, research and practice* (pp. 83–110). New York: Springer-Verlag.

Schunk, D.H. (1990). Goal setting and self-efficacy during self-regulated learning. *Educational Psychologist, 25,* 70–86.

Scott, E. & McCollum, H. (1993). Gender in classroom and school policy. In S. Biklen & D. Pollard (Eds.), *Gender and education ninety-second yearbook of the national society for the study of education: Part I* (Chapter 10). Chicago: University of Chicago.

Seeman, J. (1988). The rediscovery of the self in American psychology. *Person-Centered Review, 3,* 145–165.

Seligman, M.E. (1975). *Helplessness: On depression, development, and death.* San Francisco: W.H. Freeman.

Seligman, M.E. (1990). *Learned optimism.* New York: Alfred A. Knopf.

Sergiovanni, T.J. (1992). *Moral leadership: Getting to the heart of school improvement.* San Francisco: Jossey-Bass.

Sergiovanni, T.J. (1994). *Building community in schools.* San Francisco: Jossey-Bass.

Shavelson, R.J. & Marsh, H.W. (1986). On the structure of self-concept. In R. Schwarzer (Ed.), *Anxiety and cognition* (pp. 305–330). Hillsdale, NJ: Lawrence Erlbaum Associates.

Shaw, G.B. (1940). *Pygmalion.* New York: Dodd, Mead.

Silvernail, D. (1987). *Developing positive student self-concept.* Washington, DC: National Education Association.

Smith, B. (1943). *A tree grows in Brooklyn.* New York: Harper & Row.

Smith, C.F. (1987). *The effect of selected teaching practices on affective outcomes of graduate nursing students: An extension and replication.* Unpublished master's thesis, School of Nursing, The University of North Carolina at Greensboro.

Snygg, D. & Combs, A.W. (1949). *Individual behavior: A new frame of reference for psychology.* New York: Harper & Row.

Stanley, P.H. (1991a). *Asymmetry in internal dialogue, core assumptions, and counselor trainee effectiveness.* Unpublished doctoral dissertation, The University of North Carolina at Greensboro.

Stanley, P.H. (1991b). *Evaluation of the invitational education component of the STAR Project.* Funded by a subcontract with the RJR. Nabisco Next-Century-Schools Project. Unpublished report. International Alliance for Invitational Education, School of Education, The University of North Carolina at Greensboro.

Stanley, P.H. (1993). *Evaluation of the invitational education component of the RJR Nabisco Next-Century-Schools Project.* International Alliance for Invitational Education, School of Education, The University of North Carolina at Greensboro.

Stanley, P.H. & Purkey, W.W. (1994). Student self-concept-as-learner: Does invitational education make a difference? *Research in the schools,* 1–2, 15–22.

Stehle, C.F. (1990). The University of South Carolina Adjunct Instructor experience. In W.W. Purkey & J.J. Schmidt (Eds.), *Invitational learning for counseling and development* (pp. 101–110). Ann Arbor, MI: ERIC/CAPS.

Stillion, J. & Siegel, B. (1985). The intentionally inviting hierarchy. *Journal of Humanistic Education,* 9, 33–39.

Stuhr, J.J. (1993). Democracy as a way of life. In J.J. Stuhr (Ed.), *Philosophy and the reconstruction of culture: Pragmatic essays after Dewey* (pp. 37–58). Albany: State University of New York Press.

Swift J. (1726/1961). *Gulliver's travels.* New York: W.W. Norton.

Szasz, T. (1976). *Heresies.* Garden City, NY: Anchor Books.

Tabachnick, B.R. & Zeichner, K.M. (1984). The impact of the student teaching experience on the development of teacher perspectives. *Journal of Teacher Education, 35* (6) 28–36.

Taylor, S.E. (1989). *Positive illusions: Creative self-deceptions and the healthy mind.* New York: Basic Books.

Tesser, A. & Campbell, J. (1983). Self-definition and self-evaluation maintenance. (In) Suls, J. & Greenwald, A., *Psychological perspectives of the self,* Vol. 2 (pp. 1–31). Hillsdale, N.J: Lawrence Erlbaum Associates.

Thomas, A. (1982, March). *Invitational education: A framework for relating two theories to educational practice.* Paper presented at the meeting of the American Educational Research Association Convention, New York.

Turner, R.B. (1982, March). *Teacher invitations and effectiveness as reported by physical education students grades 9–12.* Paper presented at the meeting of the American Educational Research Association, New York.

Turner, R.B. (1983). *Teacher invitations and effectiveness as reported by physical education students.* Unpublished doctoral dissertation, The University of North Carolina at Greensboro.

Tyack, D. & Hansot, E. (1982). Hard times, hard choices. *Phi Delta Kappan, 63* (8), 511–515.

United States Department of Education. (1987). *What works: Research about teaching and learning* (2nd ed.). Washington, DC: Author.

United States Department of Justice. (1991). *School crime: A national crime victimization survey report* (Report No. NCJ-131645). Washington, DC: Author.

Wasicsko, M. M. (1977). *The effects of training and perceptual orientation on the reliability of perceptual inferences for selecting effective teachers.* Unpublished doctoral dissertation, University of Florida, Gainesville.

Weinstein, C.S. (1989). Teacher education students' preconceptions of teaching. *Journal of Teacher Education, 40* (2), 53–60.

Westbrook, R.B. (1991). *John Dewey and American democracy.* Ithaca, NY: Cornell University Press.

White, T.H. (1958). *The once and future king.* New York: Putnam.

Willis, B.J. (1970). The influence of teacher expectations on teachers' classroom interaction with selected children. (Doctoral dissertation, George Peabody College of Teaching, 1969). *Dissertation Abstracts International, 30* (11-A), 5072.

Wilson, J.H. (1990). The Kansas Elementary School Curriculum experience. In W.W. Purkey & J.J. Schmidt (Eds.), *Invitational learning for counseling and development* (pp. 79–88). Ann Arbor, MI: ERIC/CAPS.

Wilson, S.M. (1990). The secret garden of teacher education. *Phi Delta Kappan, 72,* 204–209.

Wirth, A.G. (1983). *Productive work in industry and school: Becoming persons again.* Lanham, MD: University Press of America.

Wirth, A.G. (1992). *Education and work for the year 2000.* San Francisco: Jossey-Bass.

Wizard of Oz. Original story by L. Frank Baum. Adapted by Horace J. Elias from the Metro-Goldwyn-Mayer file, 1939. New York: Harper & Row, copyright 1976.

Wood, G.H. (1992). *Schools that work: America's most innovative public education programs.* New York: Dutton.

Wright, K. (1993). *The challenge of technology: Action strategies for the school library media specialist.* Chicago: American Library Association.

Wylie, R.C. (1961) *The self-concept.* Lincoln: University of Nebraska Press.

Wylie, R.C. (1974). *The self-concept* (Vol. 1, rev. ed.). Lincoln: University of Nebraska Press.

Wylie, R.C. (1979). *The self-concept: Theory and research on selected topics* (Vol. 2, rev. ed.). Lincoln: University of Nebraska Press.

Youngs, B.B. (1993, January). Self-esteem in the school: More than a good feeling movement. *NASSP Bulletin, 76,* 549–566.

Zimmerman, I.L. & Allebrand, G.N. (1965). Personality characteristics and attitudes toward achievement of good and poor readers. *The Journal of Educational Research, 59,* 28–30

Zimmerman, B.J., Bandura, A. & Martinez-Pons, M. (1992). Self-motivation for academic attainment: The role of self-efficacy beliefs and personal goal setting. *American Educational Research Journal, 29,* 663–676.

Index

P

Pajares, M.F., 41, 43, 50, 103, 108
Panitch, D., 43
Patterson, C.H., 26, 27, 61, 62
Patterns of communication:
  described, 12–17
  feeling invited, 12–14
  feeling disinvited, 14–17
Peace of Mind (Liebman), 104
Perceptions:
  basis for behavior, 21–23
  defined, 22
  earned, 23–24
  reflected upon, 24
Perceptual tradition, explanation of,
  19–24
Personal behaviors, disinviting, 195
Personal behaviors, inviting, 195
Personal choice: and workers, 46–47
Personally inviting oneself, 104–106
Personally inviting others, 106–108
Peterson, P.L., 50
Phenomenal field, 21–22
Physical environments, disinviting,
  196
Physical environments, inviting, 196
Physical educators, 168–171
Piaget, J., 27
Pintrich, P.R., 40, 43
Plum, A., 62
Pollard, D., 29
Postman, N., 125
Potential: defined, 4–5
Powers, W.T., 20
Praise, 74
Prejudices, 65–66
Prillaman, A.R., 9
Professionally inviting oneself,
  108–109
  others, 110–118
Purkey, W.W., 5, 6–7, 10, 19, 21, 25, 28,
  29, 30, 33, 35, 40, 54, 62, 71, 72,
  89, 110, 130, 135, 136, 142
Pygmalion (Shaw), 25

Q

Quarles, C.L., 86
Questions: open ended, 116

R

Radd, T.R., 10
Raimy, V.C., 25
Reading behavior backwards, 71
Reed, C., 66, 103
Reflection, 24
Rejection, 79–80
Renzulli, J.S., 25
Resonating, 71
Respect, 51–52
Richard III (Shakespeare), 90
Richards, A.C., 21
Richards, F., 21
Riley, J.W., 89
Ripley, D.M., 51
Risks: in accepting invitations; 83
  in sending invitations, 82
Riter, A., 45
RJR Nabisco, 149–150
Roach, T., 51
Robertiello, R., 43
Robson, M., 42
Roderick, M., 17
Rogers, C.R., 25, 26, 71, 106
Rosenberg, M.J., 34
Rowe, M.B., 74
Ryan, R.M., 45

S

Safe schools, suggestions for, 97–102
Saint-Exupéry, A., 39
Scheffler, T., 4
Schmidt, J.J., 54, 142
Schmoker, M., 74
Schommer, M., 139
Schoenewolf, G., 43
School administrators, suggestions
  for, 172–176
School bus drivers, suggestions for,
  176–179